Media Intertextualities

Benjamins Current Topics

Special issues of established journals tend to circulate within the orbit of the subscribers of those journals. For the Benjamins Current Topics series a number of special issues of various journals have been selected containing salient topics of research with the aim of finding new audiences for topically interesting material, bringing such material to a wider readership in book format.

For an overview of all books published in this series, please see
http://benjamins.com/catalog/bct

Volume 37

Media Intertextualities
Edited by Mie Hiramoto

These materials were previously published in *Pragmatics and Society* 1:2 (2010)

Media Intertextualities

Edited by

Mie Hiramoto

National University of Singapore

John Benjamins Publishing Company

Amsterdam / Philadelphia

The paper used in this publication meets the minimum requirements of
the American National Standard for Information Sciences – Permanence
of Paper for Printed Library Materials, ANSI z39.48-1984.

Library of Congress Cataloging-in-Publication Data

Media intertextualities / edited by Mie Hiramoto.

p.   cm. (Benjamins Current Topics, ISSN 1874-0081 ; v. 37)

Includes bibliographical references and index.

1. Intertextuality. 2. Mass media and language. 3. Semiotics. 4. Discourse analysis--
      Social aspects. I. Hiramoto, Mie.

P302.45.M44   2012

302.2301'4--dc23   2012006684

ISBN 978 90 272 0256 7 (Hb ; alk. paper)

ISBN 978 90 272 7457 1 (Eb)

John Benjamins Publishing Co. · P.O. Box 36224 · 1020 ME Amsterdam · The Netherlands

John Benjamins North America · P.O. Box 27519 · Philadelphia PA 19118-0519 · USA

Table of contents

Media intertextualities

Semiotic mediation across time and space

Mie Hiramoto and Joseph Sung-Yul Park

1. Introduction

The semiotic concept of intertextuality (originally due to Mikhail Bakhtin; 1986/2006) was popularized in the West by Julia Kristeva (1980), who refers to it as various connections in form and content which bond a text to other texts; the central insight here is that each text exists in relation to other texts. She speaks of texts in terms of two axes; one is a 'horizontal axis' linking the creator and audience of a text while the other is a 'vertical axis' which links the text to other texts (Kristeva 1980:69). These two axes are connected through shared codes across time and space, meaning that every text and every meaning depends on preexisting codes. This intertextual perspective is crucial for our understanding of how media representations of speakers and languages shape many of our preconceptions of others. Mediatization of people, ideas, and discourses — that is, the process through which the media organizes and orients the perception and interpretation of social roles and values (Johnson and Ensslin 2007) — is constantly at work in our construction and interpretation of social identity. Mediatization is inherently intertextual (see Agha and Wortham 2005); the very nature of this process involves extracting the speech behavior of particular speakers or groups from a highly specific context and refracting and reshaping it to be inserted in another stream of representations (Bauman and Briggs 1990, Briggs and Bauman 1992, Silverstein and Urban 1996). For this same reason it is also dialogic; the way in which mediatized images and ideologies are interpreted by recipients ultimately contributes to the construction of more enduring stereotypes and evaluations of the speakers and languages represented through those texts (Spitulnik 1996, Inoue 2003, Agha 2007).

The intertextuality of the mediatization process is what makes the mass media quintessentially modern, as recognized in work on the constitution of national identity (Anderson 1983) and public space (Gal and Woolard 2001), and this observation is particularly apt in the current context of globalization. The world-wide reach of mass media constantly inserts images of culturally distant others and voices of the past into the 'here and now' of our discourse; hybridity associated with postmodern society and advances in media technologies facilitate greater mediatization across different genres and modalities. Thus the notion of intertextuality becomes a highly useful concept for the linguistic anthropological study of media discourse in the context of modernity, as it provides us with a tool for exploring the semiotic processes that underlie the way in which the media negotiate and reinscribe the complex relationships of identity that characterize late modern subjecthood.

First published as a Special Issue of *Pragmatics and Society*, issue 1:2 (2010), the collections of critical essays in this volume discusses our relation to the world by examining constructions of normative biases thorough our discursive practice in media discourse. This volume brings together scholars that approach media intertextuality from various perspectives and contexts, with an aim to understand the significance of semiotic mediation in modern media texts and contexts. Discourse analysis often offers explanations on how language use and social normativity influence and shape each other in media discourse by observing the structures and strategies of both written and spoken discourse. The papers in this volume form a strongly coherent body of work that addresses a broad range of issues regarding media intertextuality and language, and explores the impact of mediated communication and media discourse on social interaction. Ultimately, the articles collected here contribute to central issues that shape current pragmatic, sociolinguistic, and linguistic anthropological research, including: the specific semiotic processes involved in the circulation of characterological figures and semiotic registers across cultures, places, and languages (Agha 2007); strategies of footing (Goffman 1981), stylization (Rampton 1995, Irvine 2001), and stance-taking (Englebretson 2007, Jaffe 2009) as these are employed in media texts to negotiate the intertextual distances that separate the represented, the audience, and the institution of media; and how all of these processes contribute to the construction of relations of authenticity, authority, and legitimacy (Bucholtz and Hall 2004, 2005), mapping them onto a network of identities, positions, and ideologies, and thereby constituting a fundamental interpretive framework through which we make sense of our social world.

2.   Pragmatics, Society, and Media intertextuality

Mediatized texts are created with specific audiences in mind, and in doing so, texts must make connections to prior discourses. When such texts center around given personae, discourse practices are strategically assigned to such characters in order to constrain them to their given roles. We may understand this in terms of linguistic regimentation (Kroskrity 2000) within mediatized texts. Park (2009a: 548), identifying regimentation as one of the media's central effects, writes:

> The choice and allocation of languages and varieties for the purpose of broadcasting, for instance, is an important means through which those varieties come to be treated as bounded entities and placed within authorized hierarchies of legitimacy (Spitulnik 1998). … What we see here is a regimentation of language varieties along multiple axes such as standard/nonstandard, national/regional, polite/vulgar, refined/crude, and so on. These regimentations in turn open up a space for the articulation of the media institution's authority (Park 2009a: 548).

Regimentation of language varieties is often practiced in media discourse to allow mediatized personae to fit into expected social ideologies. In mediatized texts, certain attributes of social personae are animated and re-animated through textual encounters (see Agha, this issue). Such textual encounters, in the case of mass media discourse, attempt to reach as many members of the community as possible, where this community may be quite heterogeneous despite the existence of shared membership markers. Given the potential breadth of the audience, such creation of social persona, or 'synthetic personalization' (Fairclough 1989), must employ only the most salient or the most common aspects of the target community. For example, in media discourse, a specific language is often selected for the achievement of synthetic personalization in order to make a mass communication audience feel that they are 'thousands of identical *yous*, with attitudes, values, and preoccupations ascribed to them' (Talbot 1995: 148, emphasis original). In other words, synthetic personalization in mediated texts is a creation of tailored characters and situations which superficially highlight only the ideals of an audience or culture. This process is discussed in depth by Irvine and Gal (2000) through their explanation of the process of *erasure*, "in which ideology, in simplifying the field of linguistic practices, renders some persons or activities or sociolinguistic phenomena invisible" (Gal and Irvine 1995: 974). Gal (2005: 27) likewise mentions that generally, "erasures are forms of forgetting, denying, ignoring, or forcibly eliminating those distinctions or social facts that fail to fit the picture of the world presented by an ideology." In a similar way, this notion of erasure is closely associated with what Fairclough (2006/1999) refers to as *normalized, homogenized, and reduced* discursive practice.

Since the original publication of *Pragmatics and Society*, issue 1:2 (2010), papers that are very pertinent to this volume appeared as a special issue of *Journal of Sociolinguistics* on the sociolinguistics of performance (Bell and Gibson 2011). The papers in this publication take approaches such as stylization (Bakhtin 1981,

Rampton 1995, Coupland 2007), audience and referee design (Bell 1984, 2001), indexicality (Silverstein 2003; Eckert 2008), enregisterment (Agha 2003), and discursive culture (Bauman and Briggs 1990). Topics covered in the edited volume focus on staging language — language of performance — in popular music, a comedy performance, and movies. They all make particular relevance to the essays included in this volume. Specific shared ideas between the recently published issue of *Journal of Sociolinguistics* and this volume are concepts of 'enregisterment' and 'characterological figures' (Agha 2003) in mediated discourses and how media depend on intertexualities upon indexing attributes of characterological figures to mass audience. All in all, we understand and welcome expanding interests in media intertextualities in the field.

All of the papers presented in this volume are theoretically grounded in a close analysis of such semiotic processes, as they bring these insights to bear on their examination of various forms of media discourse. The contributions discuss semiotic mediation through a variety of mediatized texts (i.e. newspaper articles, movies, reality TV shows, anime, comedy performance, and government campaigns), highlighting certain diacritics of social personae that are animated and re-animated through textual encounters. The data encompass diverse cultural, national, and linguistic contexts, including positions of English speakers in South Korea, performance of California English by African English speakers, standard and non-standard language in Japan, Hawai'i Creole and standard English in Hawai'i, and discourse on Singapore Colloquial English, also known as Singlish, in Singaporean public domains.

3.   Overview of this issue

This volume explores five different institutional and cultural contexts in which media intertextualities are rendered into texts for wider public circulation. Joseph Park's paper considers the various ways in which interdiscursivity comes into play in the success stories of English language learning in the conservative press in South Korea. English as a symbolic resource frequently mediates relations of class, privilege, and authority, and the Korean media play an influential role in the negotiation of the place and meaning of English in South Korea (Park 2009b). His contribution identifies interdiscursivity (Agha and Wortham 2005) as an important semiotic mechanism for positioning English in modern South Korean society by illustrating the process through texts of the conservative newspapers which elucidate the privileges of a small group of Korean elites by characterizing them as successful English learners — speakers of "good English." There are certain types of English accents that are considered as models by South Korean English learners.

For example, American English is valued more than various world Englishes (e.g. Indian English or Filipino English) or non-native English. Similar to the examples described in Blommaert (2009: 256), an American English accent or native or native-like English exemplifies "good English" in South Korea. Park's data clearly demonstrate the ways in which various discourses, voices, and images are connected in the naturalization of the successful learner's "good English," ranging from spatio-temporally distant communicative events, authoritative voices of native speakers, and the social positions of power which the successful learner occupies. By offering a constructive approach to explain the interrelated processes of interdiscursivity in his data, Park's contribution outlines a general framework that could be applied to any context in which interdiscursivity involving the values of language can be found.

The next article, a study by Alexander Wahl, moves the analytic focus to popular visual media and investigates the process of stylization in *ad lib* performances of two iconic Hollywood film personae, Bill Preston and Theodore (Ted) Logan, known from *Bill and Ted's Excellent Adventure*. These film characters have come to exemplify California male slacker youth, stereotypically laid-back and easy going. In a popular reality television series, *Big Brother Africa: 3*, aired in 2008, two young African male contestants, 21-year-old Ricardo (Ricco) Venancio from Angola and 22-year-old Munyaradzi (Munya) Chidzonga from Zimbabwe, perform an imitation of the California style found in the Bill and Ted characters by drawing on many of the film's linguistic and semiotic features. The contestants achieve a representation that is coherent and stereotypical of the mediatization. Wahl claims that the contestants' stylization indexes their own globalized ideas about Californian and, more broadly, American youth. As Coupland (2001: 350) notes, "stylized utterances are often emphatic and hyperbolic realizations of their targeted styles and genres," and Wahl describes how one can project a desired identity by stylizing acts, speeches and looks through mediated texts. An undeniable element of the Bakhtinian notions of parody and double-voiced discourse is also involved here. Parody involves the speakers' appropriation of someone else's speech to serve their own purposes, thus creating a "double-voice" which can index different intentions of a speaker. Bakhtin (1986/2006: 106) states that "[o]ther's utterances can be repeated with varying degrees of reinterpretation. They can be referred to as though the interlocutor were already aware of them; they can be silently presupposed; or one's responsive reaction to them can be reflected only in the expression of one's own speech." The speakers' voice in parodic discourse is directly opposed to the other's voice; the two voices may be interpreted in two opposing ways. Like Hill's work on Mock Spanish (e.g. Hill, 1993, 1998, 2005), Wahl's brings current research on style, performance, language ideology to bear on our understanding of the complex chain of personae in mediated discourse.

Similar to Wahl's contribution, Mie Hiramoto's paper analyzes data based on popular television, in this case anime. She observes the Japanese language in the famous series *Cowboy Bebop* and argues that both normative and non-normative characters are constructed to conform to hegemonic ideals of gender, occupation, age, and race. Normative characters are represented as possessing mostly ideal traits, both visually and linguistically, as reflected in the artwork and speech depicting both "heroes" and "babes." At the same time, characters that do not conform to desirable sexual, visual, national, or age norms are rendered less than attractive and are assigned linguistic features that deviate from colloquial Standard Japanese. Kinsui's (2003; 2007) idea of *yakuwarigo* 'role language' is central to the designing of language concerning different personae in mediated texts such as anime. This assignment of linguistic registers is based on the semiotic process of iconization and erasure, as it helps the audience identify stereotypical images related to imaginary characters' roles. The idea of hegemonic masculinity or normative sexuality is well-represented in mainstream media discourse including scripted speech in movies, comics, games and anime. Lippi-Green (1997), in her investigation of Walt Disney cartoon stories, pointed out that accents or dialects mapped onto characters are demonstrative of their major traits and attributes in the stories. For example, protagonists never fail to speak Standard English despite the fact that they may come from a jungle or a desert of a non-Western land, while villains tend to speak with foreign accents even if they share their place of origin with the protagonist. All in all, conventionalized images of popular characters support associations of normative males and females with language of power, e.g. standard or gender-appropriate varieties (Lippi-Green 1997). Linguistic conformity associated with the normative ideology of gender and sexuality is easily established in mediated texts like anime through role language if one wishes to highlight compliance with the hegemonic hetero-normative ideology, as it is seen in Hiramoto's data; her analysis demonstrates how idealized language is assigned to fictional characters in *Cowboy Bebop* in order to appeal to the semiotics of desire rampant in today's society.

Through his observations of local comedy audiences in Hawai'i, Toshi Furukawa examines the construction of "local identity" by adopting an interactionally oriented framework. Ideas such as "local identity" may be highly idealized and thus may not be representative of the actual social situation in Hawai'i. Nonetheless, Hawai'i Creole, a locally spoken dialect of English, functions to build solidarity or to confirm membership among the residents, establishing their shared knowledge of local cultural practices, styles, and manners of speech. In contrast to Hawai'i residents' national or ethnic identities, local identity is of particular importance, given Hawai'i's cultural and geographical separation from the rest of the U.S. Most residents of Hawai'i prefer to label themselves with the catch-all term *local*, implying membership in more than one of Hawai'i's many ethnic and social communities (see Okamura 1994 for detailed discussion). The term "local" itself implies, given the broad range of ethnicities and cultures present in Hawai'i, that membership in the local Hawai'i community is based on criteria other than ethnicity and linguistic heritage. The Hawai'i-born historian John Rosa (2000: 101) states that local identity is "a matter of positioning oneself in relationship to power and place." It seems that such relationships to power and place are actively negotiated among the locals in Hawai'i Creole. Furukawa discusses these negotiations in the studied focus groups' discursive practices; he also demonstrates the significance of mediated membership categories such as age, place-names, and ethnicity in the interpretive process among and beyond the members of a local comedy audience. Furukawa shows how the interactions occurring in the data can be illustrative of how people talk about mediatized performances and how such interactions contribute both to the group members' interpretation of the performances as well as to reinforcing images and stereotypes they have about different people or social groups.

The issue's final article, by Michelle Lazar, draws on her research on the use of Colloquial Singapore English, widely known as Singlish, in Singapore's public campaigns and focuses on an intriguing dimension of media interdiscursivity. Like Hawai'i Creole, Singlish is the result of language contact; moreover, both of these newly emerged varieties are often stigmatized by educators for being "bad/broken English" (Park and Wee 2008; Wee 2006). The focus of Lazar's contribution is on the use of a popular television character, Phua Chu Kang, and his role as spokesperson in delivering public education messages to the general Singaporean audience in recent nation-wide campaigns aimed at changing particular social attitudes and behaviors. Phua Chu Kang was the likeable lead character of a locally produced sitcom of the same title in the late 1990s, which revolved around the life of a building contractor and his family. Infamous for speaking Singlish, the character had been publically criticized by the government for promoting "bad" English among the youth and the general public. However, it was this very character that was selected by the same government in subsequent years to address Singaporeans in various public education campaigns, notably a health campaign at the height of the SARS (Severe Acute Respiratory Syndrome) outbreak in 2003, and more recently, in 2009–10, in a public transportation courtesy campaign. Lazar's paper analyses the intertextualization of Phua Chu Kang's fictional persona into the everyday social life of Singaporeans. The author shows how, due to the pragmatic need to connect with the public audience on the level of mediatized personae, adoption of the previously condemned Singlish-speaking character becomes a viable strategy for the government.

This volume concludes with a commentary on each contribution by Asif Agha from the point of view of media intertextualities or "recycling mediatized personae." Agha points out how each of the contributions offers a different vantage point on the ways in which media intertextuality comes into being, and on what it accomplishes for its architects; he suggests that the authors' shared focus on competing language ideologies in the media demonstrates the extent to which the indexicality of language is currently subject to fluctuation.

Acknowledgements

This theme volume that originally appeared in *Pragmatics and Society* issue 1:2 (2010) developed from a panel presentation 'Media intertextualities: semiotic mediation across time and space' held as a part of the 108th American Anthropological Association's Annual Meeting in Philadelphia in December, 2009. Most of the papers were originally presented there; we thank the members of the audience for their enthusiastic participation and contributors for transforming their interesting presentations into a fine set of articles. We are greatly indebted to Asif Agha for his commentary. Our thanks also go to Jacob Mey for his advice and assistance during the editorial process. We also acknowledge support of the acquisition editor, Isja Conen and the editorial staff, Patricia Leplae.

References

Agha, Asif. 2003. The Social Life of Cultural Value. Language and Communication 23: 231–273.
Agha, Asif. 2007. Language and Social Relations. Cambridge, U.K.: Cambridge University Press.
Agha, Asif and Stanton E. F. Wortham (eds). 2005. Discourse across Speech Events: Intertextuality and interdiscursivity in social life. Special issue of Journal of Linguistic Anthropology 15, 1.
Anderson, Benedict. 1983. Imagined Communities: Refractions on the origin and spread of nationalism. London: Verso.
Bakhtin, Mikhail M. 1981. Discourse in the Novel. In: The Dialogic Imagination, Michael Holquist, ed. Caryl Emerson and Michael Holquist (trans.), 259–422. Austn, Texas: Universitu of Texas Press.
Bakhtin, Mikhail M. 1986/2006. The Problem of Speech Genres. In: The Discourse Reader 2nd ed., eds. Adam Jaworski and Nikolas Coupland, 98–107. London and New York: Routledge.
Bauman, Richard and Charles L. Briggs. 1990. Poetics and Performance as Critical Perspectives on Language and Social Life. Annual Review of Anthropology 19: 59–88.
Bell, Allan. 1984. Styles as Audience Design. Language in Society 13:145–204.

Bell, Allan. 2001. Back in Style: Reworking audience design. In: Style and Sociolinguistic Varia-
    tion, eds. Penelope Eckert and John R. Rickford, 139–169. Cambridge, U.K.: Cambridge
    University Prss.
Bell, Allan. and Ady Gibson (eds). 2011. The Socolinguistics of Performance. Special issue of
    Journal of Sociolinguistics 15, 5.
Blommaert, Jan. 2009. A Market of Accents. Language Policy 8: 243–259.
Briggs, Charles L. and Richard Bauman. 1992. Genre, Intertextuality, and Social Power. Journal
    of Linguistic Anthropology 2 (2): 131–172.
Bucholtz, Mary and Kira Hall. 2004. Theorizing Identity in Language and Sexuality Research.
    Language in Society 33: 469–515.
Bucholtz, Mary and Kira Hall. 2005. Identity and Interaction: A sociocultural linguistic ap-
    proach. Discourse Studies 7 (4–5): 584–614.
Coupland, Nikolas. 2001. Dialect Stylization in Radio Talk. Language in Society 30: 345–357.
Coupland, Nikolas. 2007. Style: Language Variation and Identity. Cambridge, U.K.: Cambridge
    University Press.
Eckert, Penelope. 2008. Variation and the Indexical Field. Journal of Sociolinguistics 12: 453–
    476.
Englebretson, Robert (ed). 2007. Stancetaking in Discourse: Subjectivity, Evaluation, interac-
    tion. Amsterdam: John Benjamins.
Fairclough, Norman. 1989. Language and Power. London: Longman.
Fairclough, Norman. 1995. Critical Discourse Analysis. London: Longman.
Fairclough, Norman. 1999/2006. Global Capitalism and the Critical Awareness of Language,
    In: The Discourse Reader 2nd ed.,eds. Adam Jaworski and Nikolas Coupland, 146–157.
    London and New York: Routledge.
Featherstone, Mike. 1991. Consumer Culture and Postmodernism. London: Sage.
Gal, Susan and Irvine, Judith T. 1995. The Boundaries of Languages and Disciplines: How ide-
    ologies construct difference. Social Research 62: 967–1001.
Gal, Susan and Kathryn Woolard (eds). 2001. Languages and Publics: The Making of Authority.
    Manchester, U.K.: St. Jerome Publishing.
Gal, Susan. 2004. Language Ideologies Compared: Metaphors of public/private. Journal of Lin-
    guistic Anthropology 15: 23–37.
Goffman, Erving. 1981. Forms of Talk. Philadelphia: University of Pennsylvania.
Hill, Jane. 1993. Hasta La Vista, Baby: Anglo Spanish in the American southwest. Critique of
    Anthropology 13: 145–176.
Hill, Jane. 1998. Language, Race, and White Public Space. American Anthropologist 100: 680–
    689.
Hill, Jane. 2005. Intertextuality as Source and Evidence for Indirect Indexical Meanings. Journal
    of Linguistic Anthropology 15: 113–124.
Hiramoto, Mie (ed). 2010. Media intertextualities: Semiotic mediation across time and space.
    Special issue of Pragmatics and Society 1: 2.
Inoue, Miyako. 2003. Speech without a Speaking Body: 'Japanese women's language' in transla-
    tion. Language & Communication 23: 315–330.
Irvine, Judith and Susan Gal. 2000. Language Ideology and Linguistic Differentiation. In: Re-
    gimes of Language: Ideologies, polities, and identities, ed. Paul Kroskrity, 35–84. Santa Fe,
    New Mexico: School of American Research Press.

Irvine, Judith. 2001. Style as Distinctiveness: The culture and ideology of linguistic differentiation. In: Stylistic Variation in Language, eds. Penelope Eckert and John Rickford, 21–43. Cambridge: Cambridge University Press.

Jaffe, Alexandra. 2009. Entextualization, Mediatization and Authentication: Orthographic choice in media transcripts. Text & Talk 29 (5): 571–594.

Johnson, Sally and Astrid Ensslin. 2007. Language in the Media: Theory and practice. In: Language in the Media, eds. Sally Johnson and Astrid Ensslin, 3–22. London: Continuum.

Kinsui, Satoshi. 2003. Bâcharu Nihongo: Yakuwarigo no nazo (Virtual Japanese: the mystery of role-language). Tokyo: Iwanami.

Kinsui, Satoshi (ed.). 2007. Yakuwarigo Kenkyû no Chihei (Horizons of Role-language Research). Tokyo: Kuroshio.

Kristeva, Julia. 1980. Desire in Language: A semiotic approach to literature and art. New York: Columbia University Press.

Kroskrity, Paul V. 2000. Regimenting Languages: Language ideological perspectives. In: Regimes of Language: Ideologies, polities, and identities, ed. Paul V. Kroskrity, 1–34. Santa Fe, New Mexico: School of American Research Press.

Lippi-Green, Rosina. 1997. English with an Accent: Language, ideology, and discrimination in the United States. London and New York: Routledge.

Okamura, Jonathan. 1994. Why There are no Asian Americans in Hawaiʻi: The continuing significance of local identity. Social Process in Hawaiʻi 35: 161–178.

Park, Joseph Sung-Yul. 2009a. Regimenting Languages on Korean Television: Subtitles and institutional authority. Text & Talk 29 (5): 547–570.

Park, Joseph Sung-Yul. 2009b. The Local Construction of a Global Language: Ideologies of English in South Korea. Berlin: Mouton de Gruyter.

Park, Joseph Sung-Yul and Lionel Wee. 2008. Appropriating the Language of the Other: Performativity in autonomous and unified markets. Language & Communication 28: 242–257.

Rampton, Ben. 1995. Crossing: Language and ethnicity among adolescents. London: Longman.

Rosa, John P. 2000. Local Story: The Massie case narrative and the cultural production of local identity in Hawaiʻi. Amerasia Journal 26: 93–115.

Silverstein, Michael and Greg Urban (eds). 1996. Natural Histories of Discourse. Chicago: University of Chicago Press.

Silverstein, Michael. 2003. Indexical Order and the Dialectics of Sociolinguistic Life. Lanuage and Communication 23: 193–229.

Spitulnik, Debra. 1996. The Social Circulation of Media Discourse and the Mediation of Communities. In: Linguistic Anthropology: A reader, ed. Alessandro Duranti, 93–113. Malden, Massachusetts: Blackwell Wiley.

Spitulnik, Debra. 1998. Mediating Unity and Diversity: the production of language ideologies in Zambian broadcasting. In: Language Ideologies: Practice and theory, Bambi Schieffelin, Kathryn Woolard and Paul Kroskrity, eds. 163–188. Oxford: Oxford University Press.

Talbot, Mary. 1995. A Synthetic Sisterhood: False friends in a teenage magazine. In: Gender Articulated: Language and the socially constructed self, eds. Kira Hall and Mary Bucholtz, 143–165. London and New York: Routledge.

Wee, Lionel. 2006. The Semiotics of Language Ideologies in Singapore. Journal of Sociolinguistics 10: 344–361.

Images of "good English" in the Korean conservative press

Three processes of interdiscursivity

Joseph Sung-Yul Park
National University of Singapore

In South Korea, English as a symbolic resource frequently mediates relations of class, privilege, and authority, and the Korean media play a significant role in the negotiation of the place and meaning of English in the country. This paper identifies interdiscursivity (Agha and Wortham 2005) as an important semiotic mechanism for this process, and illustrates this through texts of the conservative print media which rationalize the privileges of Korean elites by representing them as successful learners of English. This paper identifies three distinct yet interrelated processes of interdiscursivity that accomplish this work. First, the process of *spatiotemporal extension* links geographically and temporally distant communicative events with the here-and-now, setting up the relevance of the English language within local social context. Second, the process of *recursivity* (Irvine and Gal 2000) reapplies global oppositional relations locally so that the linguistic legitimacy of native speakers of English comes to serve as a basis for local elites' authority. Third, the process of *mediatization* (Johnson and Ensslin 2007) allows the media institution to selectively highlight the achievements of elite learners while erasing the problems of unequal opportunities for English language learning in Korea. Together, the three interdiscursive processes in the texts naturalize the linguistic legitimacy of elite learners of English, thereby justifying and reproducing the structure of the linguistic market in which the global language of English indexes local relations of power and privilege.

1. Introduction

Interdiscursivity, or the way in which "features of discourse establish forms of connectivity across events of using discourse" (Agha 2005: 1), has become a central idea for linguistic anthropological research lately. This usage of the term varies slightly from earlier uses, such as that introduced by Norman Fairclough (1992).

Both usages build upon a more widely circulated term, *intertextuality*, famous-
ly originating from Mikhail Bakhtin's dialogic approach to voice and genre and
propagated in the West by literary scholar Julia Kristeva; both usages are fundamentally sociopolitical rather than purely textual. But while Fairclough's notion
of interdiscursivity focuses on how connectivity of texts contributes to the constitution of discourse conventions (1992:104), recent linguistic anthropological
usage underscores the meaning-making process in which language users engage
through semiotic work across social contexts. Thus, Michael Silverstein says that,
if intertextuality is "a directionally neutral state of comparability of texts in one or
another respect," interdiscursivity emphasizes the "relationship of event to event
[that] is projected from the position of the personnel — authorial and/or animat-
ing senders, responsible receivers, nonresponsible monitors, and so on — of some
particular event in respect of one or more others" (2005:7). This new understanding of interdiscursitivity, then, draws our attention to the interpretive processes
that give rise to textual relations; it refers not just to how discourses are linked
together via circulated linguistic forms or structures, but to how such interconnectedness comes to be felt and recognized by members of a community. In this
sense, interdiscursitivity offers a powerful way of linking the micro and macro aspects of linguistics and anthropology. It allows us to ask how what goes on within
a bounded speech event may have implications in historical context, ultimately
linking up with questions of power, identity, and legitimacy that are not accountable through considerations of local interactional dynamics alone (Bauman 2005).

   This revised notion of interdiscursivity has important consequences for how
we view the role of the media in shaping the value and significance of language varieties, their uses, and users. Mass media wield a significant influence on the relative positions of language varieties within a hierarchy of authority, legitimacy, and
authenticity. This has been most saliently illustrated through the establishment
of authorized national languages since the earlier days of nationalism (Anderson
1983), a process that is often mediated through the power and authority accorded
to media institutions (Park 2010a). Many scholars, however, have noted that such
valuation of authorized varieties cannot be accomplished through top-down im-
position of language ideologies and forced socialization alone (Spitulnik 1996).
What is important is the agentive process by which individuals come to associate
particular varieties with certain images and identities, thereby allowing linguistic forms to be embedded within a system of values through circulation in social
space. For this reason, interconnectedness between discourses established through
the media, which gradually adds to and complicates the images, indexical values,
and identity figures associated with a language, serves as a central mechanism for
the media's power to produce and perpetuate stereotypes about languages and
their speakers.

Asif Agha's (2007) work, for instance, shows how the standard form of British English, or Received Pronunciation (RP), has been enregistered as a valorized accent throughout the 18th and 19th centuries. What was central in the emergence of RP as a standard, Agha notes, is a series of semiotic-chain linkages — interconnected metadiscourses about accent that gradually propagated particular conceptions of prestigious ways of speaking throughout the population, connecting these conceptions with specific person-types. The discourses that constituted this semiotic chain include genres such as prescriptive linguistic works, popular guidebooks for proper social behavior, literary texts that offer vivid personified images of accents (e.g. Dickens' Uriah Heep), and mass-circulated magazines reaching a wide range of readership across social classes. Through the interconnectedness of such discourses, RP accumulated a rich social meaning as valued accent, grounded in specific characterological figures of speakerhood. Similarly, Miyako Inoue (2006) demonstrates that it is the juxtaposition of various popular figures of womanhood of the late and post-Meiji era in Japan (ranging from the modern "schoolgirl" to urban middle-class women embodying proper cultural etiquette) with commodified indexes of modernity (such as transgressive behavior, consumption of modern products, or national and imperial discourses) that gave rise to an imagination of Japanese Women's Language, which mobilized gendered ways of speaking as a basis for constructing a modern nation out of a pristine past tradition that never actually existed (see also Nakamura 2006). Here, too, the role of interdiscursivity is highlighted by the fact that this juxtaposition is in a large part achieved through a form of mass media that became increasingly popular in Japan during the late 19th and early 20th centuries, viz., the women's magazines, whose format brought together text-based reports, captioned photographs, and advertisements all into a single page, linking them through a "contingent intertextual contiguity" (Inoue 2006: 151).

While in both cases the institutional power of the mass-circulated media played an undeniable role in infusing society with a shared valuation of linguistic varieties, it is the semiotic processes of interdiscursivity, through which discourses about language come to be linked with specific images of speakers in social context, that serve as the actual basis for such valuation. In this paper, I explore this idea in greater depth, considering how interdiscursivity works to produce effects of resignification and reevaluation of language varieties in the print news media. As I have shown elsewhere (Park 2009a), analyzing semiotic processes within media texts can provide us with rich insights on how media institutions may secure their own positions as a locus of authority. Similarly in the present paper, I argue that analyzing semiotic processes in media texts can offer a deeper understanding of how particular languages may come to acquire complex social meaning and value in a sociopolitical context. What I highlight here is the semiotic processes that establish linkages across texts, discourses, and contexts — or interdiscursive processes — that are used in the print news media. Below, I discuss three general processes that are commonly utilized in media texts in a wide range of contexts — *spatiotemporal extension*, *recursivity*, and *mediatization* — and explain how, due precisely to their interdiscursive nature, they contribute to the construction of highly specific images of speakers. Observing the working of these processes, I argue, offers a framework for analyzing media texts that is sensitive to the meta-discursive mechanisms through which social meaning of languages is constructed. But before I move on, I will first outline the data I use for my discussion and the social context where they originate — the hotly contested ideological terrain of English in South Korea.

2. "Good English" in the success stories of English language learning

The media play a major role not only in reinforcing and reproducing essentialized images of national language and identity, but also in valorizing language varieties that are considered to be important due to their pragmatic value. In the context of globalization, that valorized language is often English, particularly what is perceived to be "standard English," as it is assumed to be a fundamental resource and tool for participation in the global economy. In Singapore, for instance, where a local form of English called Singlish is widely used and often seen as an expression of local identity, the media play a significant position in promulgating the importance of standard English. An official articulation of this valorization is the Speak Good English Movement, an annual campaign that has been going on since 2000; it rejects Singlish, considering it an impediment to international communication and a handicap for the nation's economic development. The Speak Good English Movement is an instance of a genre very typical of Singapore, "The Campaign," where speeches by government officials, the mass media, and policy action work together to promote in the populace a shared perspective regarding the issue in point (Bokhorst-Heng 2005; see also Lazar, this issue). Thus the media play a significant role in both problematizing Singlish and upholding the value of standard English, which is not simply presented as an English that adheres to some (exonormative) standard, but as "good English," a language inherently superior to, and more legitimate than local varieties. Similarly, in South Korea, the media are heavily involved in mediating the meaning of English; here, however, the situation is more complex, due to the different position of English in Korean society and the different relationship between the Korean media institutions and the government.

Over the past two decades, despite the prevalent monolingualism of South Korean (henceforth Korean) society, English has emerged as a powerful symbolic resource mediating relations of class, privilege, and legitimacy. Since the country's initiation of its globalization drive in the 1990s and its neoliberal reforms of corporate governance and society in general (Kim 2000, Song 2009), English has been considered one of the key symbolic resources that indicate one's preparedness for competition in the global market. For this reason, English language skills have been used extensively as a basic criterion for hiring and promotion in the white-collar job market. This has deep implications for the reproduction of class structure, as access to better opportunities for learning English is frequently constrained by the material resources at one's disposal. Strategies for English language learning that are widely believed to be the most effective in inculcating marketable competence in English are often the most expensive ones; these include studying abroad at an early age in an English-speaking country (called *jogi yuhak*, or 'early study abroad')[1] or attending language schools with native-speaker teachers, all of which can be prohibitively costly for working class families and even for middle class families. Yet such strategies are increasingly popular among many Korean families who struggle to secure the best opportunities for their children's future (Park 2009b).

In this regard, English necessarily becomes a site of class-based tension, and what is at stake is both the notion itself of "good English" — the type of English that provides maximal value in the linguistic market — and the allocation of legitimate ownership claims to this valued commodity. It is obvious that the idea of "good English" is not a matter of objective definition. Such an evaluation can only be made ideologically from highly specific subject positions, just as the notion of "native speaker" is a discursive construct (Coulmas 1981, Rampton 1990, Widdowson 1994, Norton 1997, Brutt-Griffler and Samimy 2001, Bhatt 2002, Holliday 2005, among others). If the idea of "good English" must be imagined and constructed through language ideological work by various social actors in interaction with each other, it is precisely through this discursive work that English comes to mediate and constrain the relations of class and power in Korean society, conferring upon some the legitimacy as speakers of "good English" while rejecting others as lacking marketable linguistic skills.

And this is where the media play a key role. The Korean conservative press is a powerful agent in the construction of "good English." In particular, the three biggest newspapers in Korea, *Chosun Ilbo*, *Joongang Ilbo*, and *Donga Ilbo* (collectively known as *Cho-Joong-Dong* and taking up more than 75% of the market share; An 2006), are most notably involved in producing and circulating the dominant discourse of English in Korean society. These newspapers are highly conservative in their stances, in the sense that they are closely tied to, and strongly defend, the status quo interests and positions of the elite consisting of the bureaucracy, the

---

1. Transliteration of Korean follows the Revised Romanization system.

capitalist class, and conservative intellectuals (Kang 2005). Strongly committed to the neoliberalist ideology, the conservative press also participates actively in the promotion of English as a fundamental necessity for national competitiveness. For instance, throughout 2000, *Chosun Ilbo* ran a series titled *yeongeoga gyeongjaeng-lyeokida* 'English is Competitiveness,' lamenting Korea's incompetence on the globalized language scene, and campaigning for greater investments in methods and infrastructures advancing effective English language learning.

Part of such discourse of the conservative press is a genre that I have called elsewhere "success stories of English language learning": accounts of how a Korean person has become successful in acquiring competence in "good English" (Park 2010b). While such articles are not extremely frequent, they quite regularly feature in the conservative press's discourse on English (I have collected 60 such articles that have appeared between 1999 and 2007, which formed the basis for the analysis presented in this article; see Park 2010b for details). For instance, a salient part of the campaign "English is Competitiveness", mentioned above, was a series of articles titled *yeongeoui dalin* 'Masters of English,' which reported on 23 different successful learners of English. A large part of what texts belonging to this genre do is to define the kind of English attained by those successful learners in value-laden terms, such as *yuchanghan yeongeo* 'fluent English,' *gogeupseuleoun yeongeo* 'high-quality English,' *jeongtong yeongeo* 'legitimate English,' *wanbyeokhan yeongeo* 'perfect English,' *salaissneun yeongeo* 'living English,' and so on, all of which are implicationally positioned as "good English" (see Table 1). This constitution of "good English," in turn, provides justification for the socially privileged position of the successful learners, who are typically depicted as coming from the powerful class of social elites. In this way, the success stories work to rationalize the structure of class relations in Korean society and to reify the importance of English.

But the construction of "good English" does not depend on such metalinguistic labels alone. In this process, interdiscursivity plays a significant role. What I want to highlight in this paper is how the semiotic mechanism of interdiscursivity is exploited in the success stories of English language learning, thus serving as a primary means through which the English of the featured learner comes to be constructed as "good." The success stories I present here, I argue, are a particularly powerful illustration of how interdiscursivity achieves this effect. Through interdiscursivity, individual readers' experiences of English language learning come to be positioned as forming a discourse that is continuous with the time-space represented in the success stories; in this way, the conditions that apply to the evaluation of the featured learner's English in those public accounts are generalized, and transformed into a highly naturalized set of criteria that "define" what "good English" consists of. Due to the historical and spatial groundedness of the texts in (reportedly) actual life-worlds, this interdiscursivity also assigns the label "good

Table 1. Labels given to the English of successful learners in the data

(a)	*yuchanghan yeongeo*	'fluent English'
	maekkeuleoun yeongeo	'smooth English'
	geochimeopsneun yeongeo	'unfaltering English'
(b)	*gogeupseuleoun/gogeup yeongeo*	'high-quality English'
	pumwiissneun/pumgyeok yeongeo	'classy English'
	sujunissneun yeongeo	'high-standard English'
	jeongtong yeongeo	'legitimate English'
(c)	*jeonghwakhan yeongeo*	'correct English'
	wanbyeokhan yeongeo	'perfect English'
(d)	*san/salaissneun yeongeo*	'living English'
	siljeon/silmu yeongeo	'practical English'
	saenghwal hyeonjang yeongeo	'everyday-life situation English'
(e)	*swiun yeongeo*	'easy English'
	gandanhan/gangyeolhan yeongeo	'simple English'

English" to the language used by specific characterological person-types (Agha 2007), thus further giving such English a more material, and thereby more natural, existence. But at the same time, the "naturalization" of such characterological figures is also an outcome of semiotic chains that establish connections among various discourses and contexts to the text in question. In the rest of this article, I will discuss the three distinct, yet interrelated processes of interdiscursivity that accomplish this work of naturalization.

3. Interdiscursive processes in the success stories

3.1 Spatiotemporal extension

The first of the three processes is what I call *spatiotemporal extension* — how actions and events at distant places or in the past are invoked and connected with the present, so that what unfolds in the other time-space is made relevant to the present time-space. Spatiotemporal extension is in fact a characteristic of all news media texts. On one level, such texts always report on, and thus make reference to, what happened in the past at some (other) place, viewing it from the reporter's or journalist's present spatio-temporal position, and thereby placing those prior and distant events within a particular field of meaning. On another level, by consuming those texts, the readers engage with the texts and make sense of them in yet another time-space, grounded in the reader's here-and-now, thereby adding another layer of significance through their participation in a long chain of textual consumption and semiosis (Silverstein 2003). Thus, the meaning of the reported events or characters is ultimately created through a *string of interdiscursivity* — the way that different time-spaces are linked up with each other in particular ways.

As instances of news media texts, the success stories of English language learning therefore involve spatiotemporal extension, in the sense that they report on the successful learner who is located at a time-space different from that of the journalist or the reader. But the stories also frequently make reference to communicative events geographically and temporally distant from the successful learner's present time-space, using such events to provide evidence of the positive characteristics of the learner's English. As the events are presented as having a continuing connection with, and relevance to, the present, the stories establish continuity between those events and the reader's discursive space, thereby inculcating in the reader expectations about what "good English" is supposed to look (or sound) like. In such cases, the connectivity between these discourses is represented as a connectivity that is naturally present in the physical world; this in turn justifies the relevance of such evaluative contexts to the reader's present.

For instance, the stories frequently cite evaluations by other people, particularly by those with the authority and legitimacy to judge the quality of the learner's English — "native speakers" of English. One example is shown in (1) below, taken from an article about Han Deok-Su, a high-ranking diplomat and trade negotiator, who later rose to the position of prime minister and, as of 2010, functions as the South Korean ambassador to the United States. In the article, Han's English is praised as a "high-quality English" (*gogeupseuleoun yeongeo*) which conveys sophisticated meaning with "simple words" (*swiun daneo*). The text makes clear what such terms imply: unlike most Koreans' English which is often assumed to rely too much on complicated words, acquired through rote memorization and thus creating a contrived feeling, Han skillfully adopts basic lexical items to produce a more naturalistic and authentic, yet sophisticated style of English. This also automatically distinguishes Han's English from, say, the "simple" English that might be used by street vendors or bar hostesses who cater to US military personnel stationed in Korea.[2]

---

2. All translations from Korean are mine. Underlined portions in examples indicate English in the original.

(1) Ms. Barshefsky, the U.S. Trade Representative, asked Mr. Han at the
negotiation table, "where did you learn such high-quality English
(*gogeupseuleoun yeongeo*)?" She was so surprised that she almost fainted
(*gijeolhal jeongdolo nollassda*) when Han answered he studied by himself.
Mr. Han is well-known for using expressions such as "<u>too much to ask</u>"
instead of the Korean style "<u>demand</u>" when pointing out heavy demands
from the U.S. In particular, he uses simple words (*swiun daneo*) such as "<u>get,
take, appear</u>" freely, using them at appropriate places. Mr. Brown, ex-chief
of AMCHAM [American Chamber of Commerce in Korea], says, […] "Mr.
Han uses the expression "<u>do not sit on the fence</u>" to argue that we should not
neglect a situation; this is a very high-quality expression (*gogeupseuleoun
pyohyeon*) even for Americans." [*Chosun Ilbo*, February 4, 2000]

In praising Han's English, the article invokes speech events beyond the reporting
here-and-now. The particular event involving Barshefsky's reaction at the negotiation table gives groundedness to the assessment of Han's English as "high-quality"
English, aided by the specific materiality of the context in which the assessment
supposedly occurred, as well as by the affective response attributed to Barshefsky
— that she was so surprised at the quality of Han's English that she "almost fainted"
(a common hyperbolic expression in Korean). Similarly, the evaluative statement
attributed to Mr. Brown is also cited to testify to the authenticity of Han's English
for the Korean readers, who (in the newspaper's view) are not supposed to have
the capacity to recognize the value of Han's English. Brown's English-sounding
name and his position as former head of an important business organization again
provide serious grounding to the reported speech event; it is implied that Han's
English is valued *where* it really matters (in the realm of international economic
relations), as well as by those *who* really matter (native speakers who occupy important positions), and therefore, it must be legitimate. The interdiscursive power
of such distant speech events can be seen from the fact that the reported evaluation actually doesn't make much sense; "do not sit on the fence" is a quite casual
English idiom, not something an American English speaker would characterize
as a "high-quality expression" (which is in itself an odd comment to make). This
makes us suspect that Brown's utterance, if something to the same effect was indeed spoken, has been significantly refracted through the journalist's reporting
prism. Nonetheless, for the average Korean reader, the apparent groundedness of
the reported event is sufficient to imbue it with considerable importance and to
transform it into evidence of Han's "good English."

The communicative events invoked in the stories may not necessarily be statements about the featured learner's good skills in English. Often, the learner's *failure*
to use English in his or her earlier days of language learning is invoked as well.
Such reports work to illustrate what drove the learner to actively pursue English,

thereby characterizing the underlying quality of his or her English. In example (2), an event recounted by Sim Itaek, Chief Operating Officer of Korean Air, is reported as an explanation of how he came to value "simple and condensed English expressions." In this event, his wordy and grammatically complex sentence failed to communicate, while a much simpler utterance by an "American" apparently worked.

(2)   He continuously studies and memorizes simple and condensed English expressions [*gangyeolhago hamchukjeokin yeongeo pyohyeon*]. "Twenty years ago, I was at the airport in Phoenix, U.S. I was on the stand-by list and my seating was being delayed. Meaning to say "Would I be able to get a seat on the next flight?", I asked the American counter staff, "<u>What do you think if I will be able to be on board in your next flight</u>?" but he kept saying "<u>What?</u>" "<u>Pardon?</u>" and could not understand me. Then, an American who was in the same situation asked the staff, "<u>What about the chance?</u>" I was so shocked." [*Chosun Ilbo*, Apr 7, 2000]

Similar to Brown's evaluation in (1) above, we can again note that the utterance of the "American" is not an expression germane to the context; perhaps what the person really said was something like "What are the chances?"; perhaps the speaker was not even an "American" to begin with. In any case, this example shows how the juxtaposition of a reported event onto a present one is presented as sufficient (and powerful) ground for rationalizing the necessity of "simple and condensed English"; it is presented as unchallengable and "shocking" evidence that Koreans' awkward and contrived English does not work in real-world communicative contexts, and that what counts as "good English" is well beyond the imagination of "ordinary" Koreans.

Examples (1) and (2) show how the stories interdiscursively link geographically and temporally distant communicative events with the present, thus setting up the relevance of the English language within a local social context, and justifying the value of the featured learner's English. The stories quoted serve multiple purposes. First, they address the question of why Koreans, whose monolingual life apparently does not require them to be fluent in English, should bother to acquire "good English." As contexts in which "good English" does matter are brought into the readers' time-space via these stories, the readers are told that "good English" is never irrelevant — and that not having it brings serious inconvenience and embarrassment. Second, the spatiotemporal extension practiced in the texts also positions the successful learner at places that matter, indexing the desired global, cosmopolitan character of the learner. The stories transparently show how the successful learner has been interacting and communicating with important people at relevant places, in this way obtaining a first-hand experience of what it means to learn "good English." Third, it brings in the voices of legitimate speakers, or native

speakers of English, as the authoritative voices of evaluation. While such speakers are ideologically positioned outside of Korea, the stories bring their viewpoint
to the reader's world, making the native speaker (despite their constant absence)
forever relevant monitors of Koreans' English language skills. Through spatiotemporal extension, the ideology of *native-speakerism*, an ideology which views white,
modern, Western speakers as legitimate purveyors of English (Holliday 2005), is
given specific material shape — in the current time-space of the Korean readers.
All of these three outcomes of spatiotemporal extension set the stage for the next
process to be considered.

3.2 Recursivity

The second process is *recursivity* (Irvine and Gal 2000), in which a semiotic contrast in one domain is reapplied in another, as in cases where contrasting sociolinguistic forms that index inter-group difference may also be used by a single
speaker to index a shift in social context. But for Irvine and Gal, recursivity is not
simply about recycling linguistic resources, but a way of rationalizing structures
of power by reapplying models of hierarchical relations from one context to another. For instance, the 19th century European ethnographers discussed by Irvine
and Gal extended their ideological view of the relationship between Europe and
Africa (civilized and sophisticated Europe vs. primitive and backwards Africa) to
the internal relationships among African languages and cultures; they did this by
imposing such hierarchical oppositions to African intergroup relations (for instance, light-skinned, Islamic Fula oppressing dark-skinned, 'primitive' Sereer),
and by understanding Africa in terms of a history of conflict and conquest, which
in turn served as an important basis for justifying Europe's imperialist interven-
tion (Irvine and Gal 2000: 53–54). Since recursivity involves establishing parallels
between two different scales of social relations mediated by discourse (in this case,
one between Europe and Africa, another between African cultures), this is yet another way in which interdiscursivity becomes semiotically manifest.

   In the success stories, too, we find a recursive application of global oppositional relations of authority onto a local level, so that the linguistic legitimacy of
(white) native speakers of English comes to serve as a semiotic basis for the successful learner's authority over English in local context. The two examples above,
(1) and (2), illustrate this process. In the reported events of the stories, native
speakers or "Americans" serve as voices of authority that assess the English of the
featured learner, who is the object of their evaluative gaze. The relationship between the two is defined as one of differential legitimacy: the legitimate native
speaker vs. the Korean, the latter gaining legitimacy only upon its conferral by the
native speaker. This distinction is further naturalized by constructing the Koreans

as having qualitatively different knowledge of, and competence in, English. Both (1) and (2) above suggest that "good English" is not so much about knowing and memorizing obscure vocabulary items and complex grammatical structure (Koreans are commonly criticized for being obsessed with such things) as it is about being able to freely use colloquial expressions (such as "too much to ask" or "do not sit on the fence"), whose well-formedness can be judged only by native speakers. Competence in "good English" in this sense is inherently inaccessible to non-native speakers; thus it becomes highly "surprising" when a Korean demonstrates such competence. But even successful learners need to have their competence verified by native speakers, and through such verifications the success stories reproduce the hierarchy of legitimacy between the native speaker and the successful learner. When these stories are read by the readers, however, the same opposition of legitimacy recursively applies between the featured learner and the reader. Now, the featured learner, who is assigned the legitimacy as a speaker of "good English" by the authority vested in the native speaker, stands in a relationship of superior authority to the average Korean reader, who is deemed to be lacking in any linguistic authority with respect to English.

This recursivity, the parallel application of distinctions in legitimacy, thus plays a central role in imbuing the figure of the successful learner with authority. This is best illustrated through examples in which the successful learner provides various forms of advice to the reader regarding how they should improve their English and what they should watch out for when they try to speak English. Such advice is an important element of the success stories, and offering such advice naturally places the successful learner in a position of authority, which in turn discursively refers back to the authority of the native speaker. In example (3), Han Seungju, professor of political science at Korea University and former Foreign Minister, emphasizes the importance of "correct English" and advises the learner to make a serious effort to produce grammatically precise sentences so as to elicit the respect of "foreigners."

> (3)   What Professor Han emphasizes most is using correct English (*jeonghwakhan yeongeo*). "When you speak with a foreigner and use a plural instead of a singular, or use the wrong tense, you should not let it pass. You must correct it [on the spot] so that the other person would acknowledge, "Oh, this person really knows English." This way, your English will also improve." (*Chosun Ilbo*, March 3, 2000)

Similarly, in (4), An Jeong-Hyo, a successful novelist and translator, warns the reader to avoid *Konglish* (a blend of 'Korean' and 'English'). This popular term is used as a pejorative label for Koreanized English forms, and though exactly what constitutes Konglish is debatable, it is generally assumed to refer to the "broken"

English that arises from interference from Korean and a superficial training in English. In An's view, Konglish includes forms such as *mania* 'avid fan' or *fighting*, a cheering yell at sports events. He rejects users of these terms as "stupid" (*kkol-kapseul tteolgo*), and explains the correct usage according to native speakers' (or "Westerners'") norms.

> (4) "The English words we commonly use, the words that appear on television or novels, there are a lot of problems with these. [...] *Mania* is used to refer to a crazy person, like a person who carries a knife on the subway and kills people. It's a word that has a very negative sense. But on television, people stupidly say (*kkolkapseul tteolgo*), "so, you're a *mania* ['an avid fan']?" More than 80 percent of the English on television is like this. The worst is *fighting*. *Fighting* just means 'fighting,' like getting into a fistfight. But when we're cheering at a sports game, we say *fighting*, don't we? Westerners say, "go, go, go," in such situations." [*Sindonga*, June 1999]

In both cases, the successful learner not only offers authoritative advice on learning or using English, but also condemns the practices of ordinary Koreans — they speak in "incorrect" English to foreigners, thereby inviting negative evaluations and missing an opportunity to improve their English; and they use broken English, totally oblivious to the absurd meaning they are producing. Such stances imply a hierarchy of authority; like a teacher reprimanding a student, the successful learner criticizes Koreans using Konglish, and thereby claims a position as a competent and legitimate speaker of English while constructing the reader as a helplessly incompetent learner.

Here, the process of recursivity can be seen at work in the way the featured learner takes up imagined speech events — or purported claims about a white native speaker's perspective — and reinserts those into their interaction with the reader. When giving out their advice, the successful learners often make reference to what a native speaker would say about Koreans' English, thus mixing the voice of the successful learner with that of the native speaker to produce a heteroglossic statement which "laminates" the native speaker's authority onto the successful learner's advice (cf. Bakhtin 1981). The problematic nature of this appropriation becomes clear when we consider the fact that not all native speakers would endorse the stance attributed to them in (3) or (4) above. For instance, many foreigners living or working in Korea are likely to become familiar with such localized English expressions, and may in fact adopt them as part of their linguistic repertoire for the purpose of communicating with Koreans, rather than reject them outright as "stupid." While it is really the successful learner who is admonishing Koreans for their "bad English," the interdiscursive embedding of the native speaker's voice transforms the successful learner's stance into authoritative advice, positioning the successful learner as legitimate speaker, and the readers as willful admirers of such legitimacy.

As we can see, interdiscursive connections are at the heart of this process. With the aid of spatiotemporal extension, the linguistic authority of the native speaker is brought into the present discourse, which serves as a semiotic model for constructing the authority of the successful learner. The successful learner now enjoys every right that belongs to the native speaker; in a Korean context, he or she has the authority to judge what is acceptable or unacceptable in speaking English, to find fault with widespread linguistic practices, and to enlighten the readers about what native speakers really say. Through the process of recursivity, the successful learner becomes the native speaker incarnate, who channels the native speaker's authority, despite the latter's absence, into the ideological field of South Korea.

3.3 Mediatization

The third process is that of *mediatization*, which focuses on the "organizational and orientational role performed by the media with respect to mutual perception, the allocation and adoption of diverse social roles, and human communication in general" (Johnson and Ensslin 2007:13; see also Jaffe 2009). All media texts are outcomes of the interpretive and representational choices (Green, Franquiz, and Dixon 1997) made by media institutions and producers, as to who and what deserves coverage; in addition, how persons and events will be represented in the media is always a matter of aligning with certain worldviews and preferring some to others. Mediatization is involved in both processes discussed above, as they constitute a selective highlighting of particular events, speakers, and relations. Highlighting, as a "semiotic act that brings to salience some aspect of the social situation" (Bucholtz and Hall 2004:495; see also Park 2010b), works in tandem with erasure (Irvine and Gal 2000) to arrive at a selective, particular vision of the world (which is essentially what any media text does in representing its subjects).

In the case of the success stories, the two processes of spatiotemporal extension and recursivity jointly work to highlight specific kinds of people and discourses, packaging them into a coherent genre of media texts and putting them into circulation, while downplaying and ignoring others. For instance, the Korean discourse that valorizes English and native accents coexists with negative attitudes towards a too eager adoption of native-like pronunciation, or towards speaking positively of one's own English language skills (Park 2009b); however, while the former, positive stance forms the fundamental basis for the success stories, the latter, negative one is rarely, if ever, acknowledged in the texts. Mediatization of successful learners into success stories, then, involves a selective zooming in onto particular discourses and crafting them into coherent stories (as opposed to partial pictures). As this is a process through which structured relations between existing discourses and a genre of media texts are established, it is yet another way for interdiscursivity to figure in the success stories. In the present section, I discuss this aspect of interdiscursivity in the data by focusing on how the success stories connect with the discourse of neoliberalism dominant in contemporary Korean society.

Elsewhere, I have argued that the success stories contribute significantly to the valorization of English in Korea by functioning as tales of neoliberal personhood (Park 2010b); the following discussion briefly summarizes my argument there and relates this to our discussion of interdiscursivity. Under the neoliberal economy, a particular type of subject comes to be celebrated as the ideal worker — the person who willfully engages in projects of constant self-development and self-improvement, maximizing his or her value as human capital (Abelmann, Park, and Kim 2009, Rose 1996, Urciuoli 2008). The valorization of such modes of subjectivity supports the values upheld in the neoliberal market: unfettered competition, individual responsibility, entrepreneurial spirit, and rejection of collectivity. In this way, the ideal worker comes to internalize the belief that one should not rely on past achievements (such as academic degrees) or structures of solidarity (such as organized labor), but instead constantly strive to improve and develop oneself as a valuable resource in the free market. The characterological figure that is constructed through the success stories replicates this view within the linguistic domain, as the successful learners are represented as learners who have achieved their good competence in English through never-ending efforts at improving their ability in the language; consequently, they enjoy great social success due to their hard-earned linguistic skills. In other words, the mediatization of successful learners through the success stories connects the neoliberal discourse of self-development to accounts of English language learning, setting up a semiotic chain that invites readers to apply the images of neoliberal personhood in their valuation of the successful learners they are reading about.

The same point can be illustrated by considering whom the success stories select as their protagonists. The successful learners in the data are almost always socially successful elites. The majority of the stories are about academics (e.g., professors at elite schools, such as Yonsei University and Korea University), journalists (e.g., reporters for the Korean offices of CNN and Bloomberg), high-ranking government officials (e.g., ministers and diplomats), and top-level managers of major corporations (e.g., CEOs of companies such as LG and Korean Air), all of whom use their competence in English to carry out their important jobs with professional savvy, and interact with "native speakers" gaining their trust. In other words, an iconic link (Irvine and Gal 2000) is established between competence in English and social success; masters of English are also masters of their respective fields. While one might be tempted to take this as an illustration of the structure of the Korean linguistic market, in which people with better competence in English have better access to better jobs, I suggest that this should rather be considered an outcome of the semiotic process of highlighting, as it is also clear that access to better jobs is constrained by conditions that are considerably more complicated than the simple question of who speaks English well. The constant focus on elite learners of English and their juxtaposition with the construct of "good English," then, amounts to a constitution of a particular person-type (Agha 2007). In other words, the image of "good English" created and circulated through the success stories is mediatized as being essentially tied to the elite learner of English, as "success" in the socio-economic domain and "success" in language acquisition are conflated and presented as iconically linked to each other.

But the success stories do not stop at establishing a connection between elite language learners and "good English." It further calibrates the figure of the successful learner so that it aligns more perfectly with the image of neoliberal personhood. While successful learners are predominantly represented as social elites, the importance of their elite status for their acquisition of English is constantly downplayed; for instance, it is often explicitly denied that the experience of living overseas, which a learner has enjoyed due to his or her privileged class background, may have contributed to their good competence in English. This is noteworthy because in Korea, it is widely agreed on, even by people who cannot afford to go abroad, that living overseas is practically indispensable if one is to acquire fluency in English, particularly a "native-like" accent — which is precisely the motivation behind the heated market for *jogi yuhak* discussed above. Instead, the success stories commonly emphasize how successful learners have refused to rely on the opportunities that derive from their class privilege, and instead dedicated their individual, nearly superhuman efforts to further developing their English language skills. Thus, the success stories are full of accounts of the extraordinary effort the successful learner has put into improving his or her English, such as studying English for several hours every day, keeping notes of, and memorizing important English expressions, and participating in many English-speaking activities. The image of the successful learner who is never content with the current competence he or she has acquired and constantly strives to strengthen it, justifies their elite position; the successful learner is a "worthy achiever" who earned good competence through continuous self-improvement, not owing to any unfair, class-based privileges (see Park 2010b for details).

As we can see, the construction of the successful learner is closely linked with the construction of his or her competence, which in turn is deeply embedded in the neoliberal discourse of ideal subject positions. Through the process of mediatization, particular aspects of successful learners are highlighted, while others are erased (Irvine and Gal 2000), in order to align the figure of the successful learner more closely with the image of neoliberal personhood. In this process, successful learners come to be praised not only for their English language skills, but also for their moral character and entrepreneurial spirit, and in this way, become ideal person-types, not only with respect to linguistic skills but also as valued moral human beings. Mediatization in the context of the conservative press, which positions the success stories within the broader discourse of neoliberal human capital development, then, plays a critical role in refining the characterological figure of the successful learner. Through a neoliberal framing of the success stories, the semiotic chain of interdiscursivity is further extended, filling the figure of the successful learner with more specific traits, all of which are rooted in the neoliberal ideal of individual personhood.

4. Conclusions

I opened this paper with a discussion of how the power of media texts to shape our understanding of language and its users must be seen as emanating not simply from the institutions that produce and circulate them, but also from the interaction of such texts with a wide range of discursive and sociopolitical contexts — that is, the interdiscursivity through which those texts come to be linked with, and positioned against, other texts. Through the discussion above, I have tried to show the various ways in which interdiscursivity comes into play in the success stories of English language learning. Various discourses, voices, and images are linked together in the valorization of the successful learner's "good English," ranging from spatio-temporally distant communicative events, authoritative voices of native speakers, and images of the neoliberal subjects who enthusiastically engage in endless projects of self-development to maximize the value of their own human capital. Through these processes, the stories' readers come to position English within a set of discourses and social relations and naturalize the evaluation of the elite language learners' English as "good English." This leads to the implicit suppression, or erasure, of unequal social relations and privileges that must have served as the basis for the elites' social standing, including the structure of the linguistic market and regimes of power, particularly that of neoliberal competition and its discourses of human capital development. All of this is made possible by the power of interdiscursivity to cumulatively construct a highly specific characterological figure of the successful learner, who is associated with important spatiotemporal locations; who is invested with authority by native speakers; and who embodies the ideal neoliberal self — qualities that are supposedly demonstrated by perfect mastery of "good English."

I hope the discussion above has served to illustrate the power of interdiscursivity to mediate micro-level semiotic processes with macro-level social phenomena. The construction of the social meaning of language varieties is always a politically fraught process, having massive consequences for myriad aspects of social life and human conduct. In the case of Korea, the elevation of English to the status of a hegemonic global language carries serious political, economic, cultural, educational, and psychological implications that affect nearly every facet of Korean society. It is clear that such transformations cannot take place without top-down processes in which language policy, institutional power, and political-economical interests of actors play a key role. Yet for such large-scale processes to be meaningful, they need to be rooted in mechanisms by which individuals come to assess the language within a network of grounded semiotic differences. As previous studies have convincingly argued (Inoue 2006, Agha 2007), these processes are commonly tied to images of the speakers of the language and of the contexts in which the language is spoken. Interdiscursivity allows for such processes to be realized; through the semiotic chains established by the interconnectivity between discourses, the meaning of English in Korean society gains greater specificity and materiality, and the English language's status in Korea is rationalized and naturalized. Interdiscursivity, then, offers a powerful vantage point from which to critique media power. The impact of the success stories does not simply derive from the power of the conservative press (e.g. its large circulation and political influence), but from the way in which the press media link up with other dominant discourses, such as the Western-based ideology of the native speaker and the late-capitalist notion of the neoliberal self. Contesting these powerful discourses, then, must imply de-linking such connections and constructing alternative ones — connections which may reframe what we mean by "good English" and who we take to be a legitimate speaker of English.

Acknowledgements

I thank Mie Hiramoto for her hard work in putting together this special issue and the detailed and useful feedback she provided for this article. I also thank Agnes Kang for comments on an earlier version, and the reviewer for *Pragmatics and Society* for the insightful suggestions that helped me improve the content and presentation of this article.

References

Abelmann, Nancy, So Jin Park, and Hyunhee Kim. 2009. College Rank and Neoliberal Subjectivity in South Korea: The Burden of Self-development. Inter-Asia Cultural Studies 10, 2, 229–247.

Agha, Asif. 2005. Introduction: Semiosis across Encounters. Journal of Linguistic Anthropology 15, 1, 1–5.

Agha, Asif. 2007. Language and Social Relations. Cambridge: Cambridge University Press.

An, Gyeong-suk. 2006. Balhaengbusu Jeomyuyul Jojungdong 75% Isang [Cho-Joong-Dong Market Share Over 75%]. Midieo Oneul, October 19. http://www.mediatoday.co.kr, accessed December 18, 2009.

Anderson, Benedict. 1983. Imagined Communities: Reflections on the Origin and Spread of Nationalism. London: Verso.

Bakhtin, Mikhail M. 1981. The Dialogic Imagination. Austin: University of Texas Press.

Bauman, Richard. 2005. Commentary: Indirect Indexicality, Identity, Performance: Dialogic Observations. Journal of Linguistic Anthropology 15, 1, 145–150.

Bhatt, Rakesh Mohan. 2002. Experts, Dialects, and Discourse. International Journal of Applied Linguistics 12, 74–109.

Bokhorst-Heng, Wendy D. 2005. Debating Singlish. Multilingua 24, 185–209.

Brutt-Griffler, Janina, and Keiko K. Samimy. 2001. Transcending the Nativeness Paradigm. World Englishes 20, 1, 99–106.

Bucholtz, Mary, and Kira Hall. 2004. Theorizing Identity in Language and Sexuality Research. Language in Society 33, 469–515.

Coulmas, Florian. 1981. Introduction: The Concept of Native Speaker. In: A Festschrift for Native Speaker, Florian Coulmas (ed), 1–25. The Hague: Mouton.

Fairclough, Norman. 1992. Discourse and Social Change. London: Polity Press.

Green, Judith, Maria Franquiz, and Carol Dixon. 1997. The Myth of the Objective Transcript: Transcribing as a Situated Act. TESOL Quarterly 31, 1, 172–176.

Holliday, Adrian. 2005. The Struggle to Teach English as an International Language. Oxford: Oxford University Press.

Inoue, Miyako. 2006. Vicarious Language: Gender and Linguistic Modernity in Japan. Berkeley: University of California Press.

Irvine, Judith T., and Susan Gal. 2000. Language Ideology and Linguistic Differentiation. In: Regimes of Language: Ideologies, Polities, and Identities, Paul V. Kroskrity (ed), 35–83. Santa Fe, N.M.: School of American Research Press.

Jaffe, Alexandra. 2009. Entextualization, Mediatization and Authentication: Orthographic Choice in Media Transcripts. Text & Talk 29, 5, 571–594.

Johnson, Sally, and Astrid Ensslin. 2007. Language in the Media: Theory and Practice. In: Language in the Media, Sally Johnson and Astrid Ensslin (eds), 3–22. London: Continuum.

Kang, Myung-koo. 2005 The Struggle for Press Freedom and Emergence of "Unelected" Media Power in South Korea. In: Asian Media Studies: Politics of Subjectivities, John Nguyet Erni and Siew Keng Chua (eds), 75–90. Oxford: Blackwell.

Kim, Samuel S. 2000. Korea's Segyehwa Drive: Promise versus Performance. In: Korea's Globalization, Samuel S. Kim (ed), 242–281. Cambridge: Cambridge University Press.

Nakamura, Momoko. 2006. Creating Indexicality: Schoolgirl Speech in Meiji Japan. In: The Language and Sexuality Reader, Deborah Cameron and Don Kulick (eds), 270–284. Abingdon, U.K.: Routledge.

Norton, Bonny. 1997. Language, Identity, and the Ownership of English. TESOL Quarterly 31, 3, 409–429.

Park, Joseph Sung-Yul. 2009a. Regimenting Languages on Korean Television: Subtitles and Institutional Authority. Text & Talk 29, 5, 547–570.

Park, Joseph Sung-Yul. 2009b. The Local Construction of a Global Language: Ideologies of English in South Korea. Berlin: Mouton de Gruyter.

Park, Joseph Sung-Yul. 2010a. Language Games on Korean Television: Between Globalization, Nationalism, and Authority. In: Language Ideologies and Media Discourse: Texts, Practices, Politics, Sally Johnson and Tommaso M. Milani (eds), 61–78. London: Continuum.

Park, Joseph Sung-Yul. 2010b. Naturalization of Competence and the Neoliberal Subject: Success Stories of English Language Learning in the Korean Conservative Press. Journal of Linguistic Anthropology 20, 1, 22–38.

Rampton, M. B. H. 1990. Displacing the "Native Speaker": Expertise, Affiliation, and Inheritance. ELT Journal 44, 2, 97–101.

Rose, Nikolas. 1996. Inventing Our Selves: Psychology, Power, and Personhood. London: Cambridge University Press.

Silverstein, Michael. 2003. Indexical Order and the Dialectics of Sociolinguistic Life. Language and Communication 23, 193–229.

Silverstein, Michael. 2005. Axes of Evals: Token versus Type Interdiscursivity. Journal of Linguistic Anthropology 15, 1, 6–22.

Song, Jesook. 2009. South Koreans in the Debt Crisis: The Creation of a Neoliberal Welfare Society. Durham: Duke University Press.

Spitulnik, Debra. 1996. The Social Circulation of Media Discourse and the Mediation of Communities. Journal of Linguistic Anthropology 6, 2, 161–187.

Urciuoli, Bonnie. 2008. Skills and Selves in the New Workplace. American Ethnologist 35, 211–228.

Widdowson, Henry G. 1994. The Ownership of English. TESOL Quarterly 28, 2, 377–389.

The global metastereotyping of Hollywood 'dudes'

African reality television parodies of mediatized California style

Alexander Wahl

University of California, Santa Barbara

This study investigates the phenomenon of metastereotyping — that is, the linguistic parody of stereotypic mediatized personas. The analysis draws on data from the 2008 reality television program *Big Brother Africa 3*, in which contestants ironically perform the lead characters from a 1989 Hollywood teen comedy film who exemplify a highly mediatized California male slacker youth stereotype, the 'dude' persona. By examining the linguistic and embodied features deployed by the reality show contestants in their stylization of the film characters, the article shows how metastereotyping involves forms both from within the original representation and beyond. The use by these African contestants of features with such varied semiotic trajectories reveals their globalized ideologies about California and American youth styles as well as their understanding of the film characters' positions within these styles.

1. Introduction

As has been well established by recent research in sociocultural linguistics, individuals present themselves as particular kinds of people through the styles that they draw on both in their talk and in their embodied comportment (e.g., Auer 2007; Bucholtz 2010; Coupland 2007; Eckert 2004; Irvine 2001; Johnstone et al. 2006; Mendoza-Denton 2008). These styles comprise repertoires of semiotic features that individuals selectively bundle together and deploy in interaction. The features involved in both broader repertoires and local, interactional instances of bundling are bound together as stylistically congruent by social actors' ideological understandings. However, such ideologies are not identical across individuals. Interactants must share some degree of cultural knowledge to recognize a particular semiotic representation as belonging to the same style. But even when there is such commonality, a form considered iconic of a style by one person may serve for another only as a minor index or may not index the style at all. The specific group of people who share an ideological understanding linking a feature to a style in a particular way make up the feature's "social domain" (Agha 2007: 64). While this domain accounts for a particular stylistic form's synchronic use, the form also has a diachronic trajectory along which it has arrived at its present ideological position. It is through features' intertextual trajectories of historical use by different social actors — the "speech chain networks" of these features (2007: 67) — that styles are formed and reformed, or "enregistered" (2007: 55), as ideologies and features are repeatedly deployed and contested.

Everyday face-to-face social interaction traditionally has been understood to be the primary site of such invocation and transformation of styles. When the social domain of a feature includes the speaker but not the hearer, the speaker's very use of this feature may or may not transform the hearer's ideological understanding of it. That is, the social domain could be expanded to include the hearer. In this case, the hearer might subsequently use this feature in speech of their own, further expanding the speech chain network of this feature to other social actors. Whether or not such ideological expansion takes place has to do in part with the hearer's perceptions of the speaker's authenticity and legitimacy in producing the style. Of course, such perceptions are themselves ideologically situated, so the same bundle of features deployed by a speaker in an enactment of a style could be seen as wholly congruent by one recipient while interpreted as exhibiting incongruities by another. Or, enactments of the same target style by two different speakers could be understood as equally accurate representations by one hearer while being viewed as manifesting contrastive degrees of stylistic congruence by another. Thus, the trajectories that features' speech chain networks end up taking are decided by a complicated interplay of stylistic deployments and ideological relativities, as the social domains of forms are sometimes expanded and other times limited in the halting progression of enregisterment.

The loci of interaction in which such enregisterment transpires need not reside solely in the everyday and the face-to-face, however: the post-modern mediascape (Appadurai 1990) points to an as-yet under examined level of complexity in the trajectories of features. In this semiotic sphere, mediatized enactments of style can rapidly circulate to wide audiences, a fact that holds important implications for style, ideologies, and enregisterment. The social domains of features deployed in mediatized stylistic enactments do not necessarily include every audience member. However, the institutional power of the media often may be enough to extend such social domains to include many of these recipients. It is in this way that consumers learn new style from the media. But the media are also beholden to stylistic ideologies already circulating in society: indeed, it would be bad business to produce mediatized stylistic enactments to which the majority target audience has no cultural access whatsoever. Thus, ideological understandings of the audience both inform and are created by representations of style in the media (Spitulnik 1997; cf. Urban 1991).

Furthermore, similar to everyday interaction, today's media audience may be tomorrow's producers of stylistic enactments. These enactments may draw on prior mediatized portrayals due to the advantages of shared cultural access. That is, because the broad circulation of the same mediatized images makes particular configurations of reproduceable style more recognizable across large populations, the media becomes a valuable semiotic source for interactional stylework. The mediatized semiotics drawn on by speakers may be specific forms, bundles of features, or even an entire persona: that is, an iconic representation of style that is embodied as a particular individual. But while the touchstone status of these features and personas offer them as cultural capital for everyday interactional styling, the fact that the mediatized intertextual sourcing of such features is so recognizable also lays bare their authorship by someone other than the current speaker.

In this interplay of media and everyday interaction, the discursive act of performed stylization offers a valuable resource for navigating overt intertextuality, prior authorship, and culturally prominent ideologies and stereotypes. In stylizations, speakers creatively deploy styles in such a way as to communicate to addressees that they are not speaking as themselves, but rather are taking up the voice of another (see also Lazar, this issue). Such "strategic inauthenticity," as Coupland characterizes it (2007: 154), is enacted by the particular way in which the stylized features are realized. This deauthenticating effect may be achieved largely through two semiotic processes. On the one hand, speakers may engage in hyperbole (Coupland 2007), or exaggeration of the quality and frequency of particular semiotic features. In its most extreme form, hyperbole elides the natural variation found in language use in order to populate every structurally possible site for a particular feature with this feature. On the other hand, speakers also often reduce the semiotic complexity of the stylized representation in comparison to that which is found in the 'real' style by eliminating certain features from the bundle. Such elision may involve erasure (Irvine and Gal 2000; see also Park, this issue) — that is, it may be ideologically motivated — or it may result from incomplete access to or a lack of fluency in the original source style. Furthermore, these two semiotic processes are synergistic: while the elision of features foregrounds those that remain, hyperbole backgrounds forms that are not exaggerated. Which features are hyperbolized and which are elided has to do in part with circulating ideologies about their stylistic salience. It is ultimately through the pairing of these semiotic processes, then, that the target style is ideologically reduced in the representation to a handful of stereotypic features. Ultimately, stylizations enable everyday speakers and media performers alike simultaneously to capitalize on broad audience recognizability of widely circulating voices and stereotypes and to acknowledge these texts' highly apparent prior authorship.

Previous research on stylization in media contexts has focused largely on the phenomenon of mock languages, or simplified representations of (usually) ethnoracially associated linguistic varieties. Jane Hill's (e.g., 1993; 2008) seminal work on Mock Spanish launched this domain of inquiry, and since then, other scholars have published work identifying and analyzing Mock Asian (Chun 2004), Mock Ebonics (Ronkin and Karn 1999), Mock Filipino (Labrador 2004), Mock Hollywood Injun English (Meek 2006), and mocking portrayals of white speakers' linguistic varieties by Black comedians (Rahman 2004), to name a few. Although the targeted codes in these different mock languages vary, the stylizing processes of hyperbole and elimination are consistently used to foreground ideologically salient features and background non-salient ones, thus reproducing stereotypes about these groups and their use of language. In particular, mock languages are frequently used to ideologically evaluate the speakers of the original styles as unintelligent through the different ways in which their use of the portrayed styles is naturalized.[1]

In addition to stylized production within the media, scholars have also examined the everyday use of features sourced from the media, showing how the presumption of shared access to widely circulating media allows face-to-face speakers to draw on chunks of mediatized text for particular interactional goals (Roth-Gordon 2009; Shankar 2004; Spitulnik 1997). While the research on mock languages mainly focuses on the semiotic transformations of stylized language as it is made "strategically inauthentic" in the media, these latter authors focus on the transformations in meanings that result from the recontextualization of mediatized language — which is not necessarily stylized — into everyday interaction.

The present study builds on these two bodies of work by investigating mediatized interactional stylizations of Hollywood film characters who already engender stylized personas. The analysis considers two Black African male contestants from the 2008 reality television program *Big Brother Africa 3*, Ricco and Munya, who perform spontaneous, unscripted parodies of the eponymous protagonists of the 1989 cult classic Hollywood teen comedy *Bill and Ted's Excellent Adventure*. Bill and Ted instantiate the dude persona, an adolescent, Californian male slacker character found in various 1980s-era films who is associated with the practices of surfing, skating, pot smoking, and/or rock and roll (Kiesling 2004). This persona

---

1. In Mock Ebonics, for example, African Americans are intellectually derogated for their essentialized use of hyperbolic cursing and nonstandard, unsystematic grammar (Ronkin and Karn 1999).

is in turn a stereotypic representation of white California youth, one that subverts dominant, idealized images of this group as a paragon of American suburban life.

Although Ricco and Munya specifically target Bill and Ted, the fact that the film characters' original representation is already a stereotyping of California youth means that the contestants' parody operates simultaneously on two levels. That is, their stylization stereotypes Bill and Ted at the same time that it reproduces the film characters' own stereotyping of California — or, more broadly, American — youth. This process engenders a stereotyping about stereotyping, or what I term 'metastereotyping.' A useful framework for conceptualizing this process is Silverstein's (2003) theory of indexical orders. In this approach, the indexes that link features to styles in particular contexts and for particular speakers — the pragmatics of a style — are said to be of the n-th order. From time to time, new ideological awareness of this pragmatics takes root, either among the existing users of the style or among others who are in contact with it. Crucially, this awareness may motivate a shift in the pragmatics itself. When this occurs, the new indexes that are generated are said to be of the $n + 1$st order. The recursivity inherent in Silverstein's modeling of indexical orders captures the potentially ongoing nature of this chain of pragmatic innovation and can be used to account for both stereotyping and metastereotyping. That is, while the stereotypic performance of the dude persona enacted by Bill and Ted in the film occurs at the $n + 1$st order, the reality show contestants' metastereotypic performances operate at the $n + 2$nd order. Figure 1 schematizes the relationship between these three orders.

---

n-th order : Original California source style
↓
$n + 1$st order : Film stylization stereotypic of original source style
↓
$n + 2$nd order : Reality show stylization metastereotypic of film stylization

---

Figure 1. Indexical orders in the metastereotyping of the dude persona

This schematization should not, however, be taken to mean that the semiotic trajectories of metastereotypic features across orders are all the same; a bundle of features indexing California style is not simply taken up in its entirety and stylized by Bill and Ted, and then taken up in its entirety and further stylized by Ricco and Munya. Rather, at each successive order, prior features drop out while new features, not found in previous targeted representations, are brought in. The speech chain networks of these new features may link them to sources within California style or beyond it. Therefore, as stylized features are bundled at each order across this iterative, potentially ongoing process, their different possible patterns of complex semiotic trajectories must be accounted for in order to gain a comprehensive understanding of metastereotyping. In addition to describing such patterns, I argue that, despite the innovations at each indexical order, the performed features are together construed as a congruent reproduction of the prior representations. Moreover, I argue that the partially contrastive repertoires of features drawn on by the two reality show contestants reveal their distinct ideological understandings of the targeted style and of what constitutes congruence with it. Finally, I show how these features are used by the reality show contestants in discourse to ideologically evaluate the performed personas as unintelligent and thereby position themselves within globalizing processes in relation to mediatized stereotypes of California youth and American youth generally.

2. Data

While the analytic focus of this article is the $n + 2$nd order stylization of Bill and Ted by the African reality show contestants, I include excerpts from the $n + 1$st order film representation where appropriate in order to trace the semiotic trajectories of metastereotypic features drawn on and hyperbolized — and, in some cases, elided — at the $n + 2$nd order. *Bill and Ted's Excellent Adventure* has now endured as one of the most iconic examples of Hollywood's 1980s dude films, yet its initial meteoric success was unanticipated (Lundquist 1996). As a result of its popularity, an entire franchise emerged that included a feature-length sequel, both live-action

Copyright 1989 MGM/United Artists

Figure 2. Bill S. Preston, Esq. (Alex Winter) and Ted 'Theodore' Logan (Keanu Reeves)

and cartoon television series, a comic book, and even a breakfast cereal. Its cultural salience has attracted extensive academic attention to the film as well. In addition to sociolinguistic consideration of the film's role in the enregisterment of the lexical item *dude* (Kiesling 2004), *Excellent Adventure* has received analysis in media and cultural studies for its treatment of homoeroticism (Troyer and Marchiselli 2005), its commoditization of the historical (Shary 1998), and its post-capitalist utopian vision (Lundquist 1996). The particular brand of the dude persona engendered by Bill, played by Alex Winter, and Ted, played by Keanu Reeves (see Figure 2), is that of dim-witted teenage aspiring rock musicians in Southern California who find little success in their societally prescribed roles as high school students. In order to avoid failing their history class, they travel back through time to bring famous historical figures to present-day San Dimas, California, with the purpose of including them as live props in their final presentation. Throughout these antics, Winter and Reeves stylize an array of features indexical of a particular stereotypic image of California youth. Their highly exaggerated use of these different features is clearly performed rather than part of their ordinary speech style.[2]

The reality television show that is the site of the metastereotypic representation of the Bill and Ted characters, *Big Brother Africa*, is produced by the Dutch company Endemol and is part of its international Big Brother television franchise, which began in the Netherlands in 1999. Since then, numerous versions of the show have been launched around the world, with 38 different national and 7 multinational incarnations. In November 2008, the African version completed its third season. The South African television network M-Net broadcasts the program to 42 countries across the continent. However, according to the online South African periodical Mybroadband.co.za, DStv — the satellite television provider that transmits M-Net to these international audiences — only reached 2 million subscribers continent-wide in 2007, with 1.5 million of those residing in South Africa alone (2007). And while other consumers without such televised service can view limited video content on the program's website, home Internet access in Africa is not widespread. Thus, in a continent of nearly a billion inhabitants, those who are able to participate as audience members in this example of contemporary transnational television entertainment still only make up a fraction of a percent of the total population.

The design of the program is not unlike other examples of the competitive reality television genre. The program in question brought 12 contestants together — each from a different sub-Saharan country — to live together in one house

2. Moreover, neither actor is a native Californian. Winter was born in London, raised in St. Louis, and schooled in New York City, and Reeves was born in Beirut and raised in New York City and Toronto.

in metropolitan Johannesburg for 91 days under constant camera surveillance. The contestants were not permitted to leave the house but were required to interact, complete competitive tasks, eat, and sleep under the same roof. Each week, viewers voted via cellular text messages to determine which contestant should be eliminated.

This analysis focuses on the final days of the program, when only three contestants remained: Hazel, from Malawi; Munya, from Zimbabwe; and Ricco, from Angola. The three contestants' middle-class access to institutional resources afford them native-level fluency in the respective post-colonial European languages that are the official — though not necessarily majority — tongues of their countries of origin. For Hazel and Munya, this language is English, while Ricco speaks Portuguese natively. And although he is fluent in English, his morphosyntax and, to a larger degree, his phonology show influence from Portuguese. From the larger data set of approximately 90 hours of video footage posted on the *Big Brother Africa* fan website, I analyze four different video clips spanning two days.[3] The interactions in all four clips were transcribed using the Santa Barbara transcription method (Du Bois et al. 1992; see appendix for conventions). Throughout these clips, Ricco and Munya perform spontaneous, unscripted stylizations of the Bill and Ted characters by drawing on a wide array of linguistic strategies and forms.[4] The contestants' status as members of a small educated African elite might be credited not only for their media access to the Bill and Ted film in the first place, but also for their knowledge of other features and ideologies that are stylistically congruent with the target personas.

The following is a brief characterization of each of the four clips under analysis. The titles were assigned by the producers of the television show as part of the program's online video archive. Each of these titles intertextually draws on the name of a Hollywood film or, in one case, an American rap song, and such intertextualities make reference to different aspects of the contestants' performance. However, the continuity of the contestants' stylization across all four clips makes it clear that Ricco and Munya are performing a single pair of characters rather than individually parodying each of the films cited in the clip titles. Moreover, several explicit and implicit elements of their performance reveal these characters to be Bill and Ted. All of the clips take place in the courtyard of the house where the contestants live.

---

3. The video clips were originally at http://www.bigbrotherafrica.com/ but are no longer available.

4. Although Hazel jokingly performs the role of 1970s disco star Donna Summer in order to play along with Ricco and Munya's performance, she does not in any way stylize this identity through phonological, prosodic, or lexical features. Her more minimal performance thus falls beyond the purview of this analysis.

2.1 *Spoofing Bill and Ted*: 6:40, beginning at 16:41 GMT +2, November 18, 2008

This is the first clip in which Ricco and Munya perform Bill and Ted and is the only clip in which they are seen wearing wigs, which appear to have been provided as props by the producers, perhaps to give the contestants something entertaining to do. Crucially, these wigs approximate the contestants' target personas: Ricco wears a wig resembling Ted's long straight dark brown hair, while Munya wears a wig resembling Bill's short blond curly hair. Thus, the wigs implicitly identify Bill and Ted as the target of the contestants' stylization. Moreover, this target is explicitly identified by the producers both in the title of the clip and in the caption that accompanies it: "The housemates create their own Bill and Ted's Excellent Adventures." When the clip begins, Ricco and Munya are already in character, discussing the 'marijuana' — in fact tobacco cigarettes — that they are smoking. After Hazel identifies herself as Donna Summer, the rest of the clip revolves around the two men's performed attempts to woo her.

2.2 *Pass the Courvoisier*: 1:14, beginning at 20:08 GMT +2, November 19, 2008

The following day, Ricco and Munya revive their stylized personas (Hazel is not present). The greater part of this clip does not feature the Bill and Ted personas — rather, Ricco and Munya pretend to pass an invisible soccer ball back and forth. It is only toward the end of the clip that the two break into their Bill and Ted personas as they congratulate themselves on a game well played. The title of this clip, taken from the name of a song by American rapper Busta Rhymes, seems to be a punning reference to the activity of passing a soccer ball.

2.3 *Dumb and Dumber*: 3:53, beginning at 20:19 GMT +2, November 19, 2008

Soon after the previous clip, Hazel joins the two men, and Ricco and Munya continue to stylize Bill and Ted. This clip shares its name with an eponymous 1994 Hollywood film in which two adult men of low intelligence travel to Aspen, Colorado to track down a love interest. The intertextual connection between titles seems to be motivated by the content of the clip: Hazel's declaration that she does not like to date smart men prompts a competition between Ricco and Munya, in their Bill and Ted guises, to see who is the 'dumber' of the two. The two offer various enacted and narrated physical and mental demonstrations of their stupidity. One such demonstration provides another explicit reference to the Bill and Ted target characters when Ricco claims that he himself is "so dumb that I know who, Bill, whatever his name is, is."

2.4 *Dazed and Confused*: 4:09, beginning at 20:32 GMT +2, November 19, 2008

Here, the two men, again performing Bill and Ted, discuss with Hazel their confusion regarding the distinction between surfing waves and surfing the Internet,
and Hazel provides clarification. The clip ends with the two men explaining to
Hazel that their source of money for maintaining their lifestyles is the Mafia.
Dazed and Confused is the title of a Hollywood high school coming-of-age film in
which marijuana use is foregrounded. While (lack of) intelligence seems to be the
shared theme motivating the producers' intertextual linking of film and clip titles
in *Dumb and Dumber*, it appears to be cannabis consumption that drives the link
here: Ricco and Munya frequently pretend to be smoking a joint as part of their
stylization. Although both the *Dazed and Confused* and *Dumb and Dumber* films
share salient aspects with Ricco and Munya's performance, they are not dude films
in the prototypical sense.

In the next two sections, I provide an in-depth analysis of Ricco and Munya's
stylization across these four clips. In so doing, I develop an account of the different patterns of semiotic trajectories that characterize the contestants' ideologically
selective uptake of features from the film as well as beyond.

3.   Metastereotyping features from the film

The original Bill and Ted characters stylize a vast repertoire of features at the $n +
1$st order that index stereotypes of California youth. However, as I demonstrate be-
low, the semiotic trajectories that link the representations of these features across
different indexical orders are not uniform. In some cases, a feature that is part of
the n-th order source style may first be taken up and stylized at the $n + 1$st order
of the film, and then taken up again and further stylized by the contestants at the
$n + 2$nd order. At the same time, certain features from the source style that are
taken up in the film may not undergo subsequent metastereotyping by Ricco and
Munya. Features of this type, then, would have representations at the n-th and $n
+ 1$st orders, but not at the $n + 2$nd order. Alternatively, there are other features
that are first stylized in the film and then further stylized by the contestants, but
which do not originally source from an everyday California style. Here, features
are represented at the $n + 1$st and $n + 2$nd orders, but they are not represented at
the n-th order. In the following subsections, I examine each of these taxonomic
types of semiotic trajectories.

3.1   N-th, $n + 1$st, and $n + 2$nd order representations

The lexical item *dude* exemplifies the pattern in which the same form is represented across all three orders: while it is indexical of California youth at the n-th order, it is first stylized at the $n + 1$st order in the film, and then further stylized by the reality show contestants at the $n + 2$nd order. The fact that *dude* is such an iconic index of a particular California youth style may explain this cross-representational integrity. In other words, such broad ideological accessibility makes *dude* an especially valuable resource for the (meta)stereotyping of this style.

Example 1, excerpted from the film, demonstrates an $n + 1$st order hyperbolic portrayal of *dude*. Here, Bill and Ted have traveled through time to Ancient Greece where they encounter Socrates, with whom they attempt to communicate. The characters use *dude* 3 times in 8 lines:[5]

Example 1. *Bill and Ted's Excellent Adventure*
1	TED;	All we are is dust in the wind, dude. ((TO SOCRATES))
2	BILL;	((PICKS UP DUST FROM TRAY AND THEN LETS GO))Dust.
3		((BLOWS DUST FROM HAND AND WIGGLES FINGERS)) Wind.
4	TED;	((POINTS AT SOCRATES)) Dude.
5	SOCRATES;	Ah. Ah.
6		Yes, like sands of the hourglass, so are the days of our life ((IN GREEK))
7		@@@ ((CLAPS))
8	BILL;	Let's get out of here, dude.

In turn, this feature is hyperbolized to an even greater degree in the reality program. In Ricco and Munya's joking quest to woo Hazel with their lack of intelligence in the *Dumb and Dumber* clip, the two men eventually — and ironically — concede that their efforts are to no avail, as they must not be stupid enough for her taste:

Example 2. *Dumb and Dumber*
74	MUNYA;	dude <[dud]>, … dude <[dud]>, when she says dumb,
75		she means like, the opposite of us, dude <[dɪd]>.
76		… du::de <[dɪd]>=.
77	RICCO;	=dude <[dɪd]>, we sma:rt,
78	MUNYA;	I know, dude <[dɪd]>, … #so other people are dumb.

Munya uses *dude* 5 times within this excerpt in which he utters a total of 23 words, a rate of more than one token every five words. Although Bill and Ted are frequent *dude* users, nowhere in the film does this rate of production occur. As the trajec-

---

5. The example also includes another intertextual allusion to the soap opera *Days of Our Lives*.

tory of *dude* carries it across successive indexical orders, it is increasingly hyperbolized in each stylization. This process demonstrates the ideological salience of *dude* as a stereotypic index of the stylistic target for both the contestants and the film characters. Moreover, this steadily increasing hyperbole allows prior authorship to be highlighted again and again as each order is semiotically exaggerated with respect to the immediately prior representation.

At the same time, the enactment of this n + 2nd order hyperbole is not evenly distributed between the two contestants. Rather, as seen in Example 2, it is almost solely the work of Munya, who uses 55 tokens of *dude* throughout the 895 words he utters across these four clips, an average of one token every 16 words. Ricco, in contrast, produces *dude* only six times during his 795 total words, a rate of one token every 133 words. Moreover, when he does utter *dude*, only once does it not follow a use of *dude* by Munya in an immediately prior turn. In other words, Munya is overwhelmingly the first to stylize *dude* in a particular local discourse context. Ricco occasionally then takes up and redeploys this form. This pattern is exemplified in Example 3, in which Hazel has just left the courtyard area in order to retrieve a wig for herself. In the lull in action that ensues following her departure, the silence is broken by Munya:

Example 3. *Spoofing Bill and Ted*
162 MUNYA;   Du:de <[dɨd]>,
163 RICCO;   Dude <[dud]>=,
164 MUNYA;   =Hey, what happened to that hot chick, dude <[dɨd]>?
165 RICCO;   Uh, which o:ne, dude <[dud]>=,

Ricco's uses of *dude* in lines 163 and 165 not only follow uses of *dude* by Munya, but they also clearly resonate with (Du Bois 2007) the syntactic and discursive structure of Munya's utterances on lines 162 and 164, respectively. This same interactional strategy of second-person resonance is used frequently by Ricco to stylize forms other than *dude* that are originally introduced by Munya. It is emblematic of a broader pattern in which Munya's overall stylization — and thus his ideological understanding of the style — is more congruent with Bill and Ted and with the dude persona. At the same time, the uptake of these features by Ricco enables him to hone his performance and broaden his ideological understanding of the target style while also revealing his own orientation to Munya's stylistic authority.

3.2 *N*-th and *n* + 1st order representations only

Part of *dude*'s iconic status may have to do with the fact that it can index California style not only lexically but also phonologically (Kiesling 2004). Specifically, /u/ is a target for fronting, a process that is part of the California Vowel Shift (Eckert 2010;

Hinton et al. 1987). This feature is stylized by both contestants; Ricco and Munya pronounce *dude* using a fronted vowel in Example 2 (lines 75–80); and Munya does so in Example 3 (lines 162 and 165). However, their use of stylized fronting in *dude* is not categorical, as seen in the above examples. Furthermore, other than *dude*, Ricco and Munya do not front /u/, and other phonological changes associated with the California Shift are limited to a few forms in their performance: fronting of back vowels in single tokens of *so, bro, you know, fully* and a handful of tokens of *totally* (see below), and centralization of front vowels in single tokens of *shit* and *yeah*. With the exception of *dude*, all of these cases of phonological innovation are produced by Munya, again suggesting a stylization and an ideological understanding more closely tied to the semiotic target than that of Ricco. Overall, vowel stylization for the contestants appears to be largely lexically specific, with no evidence that the stylization of vowels represents productive patterns that the contestants can apply generally to words containing particular target segments. For Ricco and Munya, then, the lack of such patterns fails to distinguish these vowels as stylized features at the $n + 2$nd order separate from the lexis in which they are embedded and on whose semiotic trajectories they are thus parasitic.

In contrast to Ricco and Munya's nonproductive vowel use, the film characters' stylized vowels are independent of the lexis, with their own speech chain networks carrying them across indexical orders. That is, the stylization of vowels in the film is widespread and not limited to particular iconic forms, and thus distinguishes the vowels as features separate from the lexis. Example 4, excerpted from the film, exemplifies this productivity, with innovative California pronunciations given below the line of script:

Example 4. *Bill and Ted's Excellent Adventure*
BILL;   I don't know Ted, but I do know we're in serious trouble.
            [θ] [æ]   [i] [θ]

Unlike Ricco and Munya, the film actors stylize nearly every potential vocalic target in their talk as the Bill and Ted characters. This difference between the film characters' treatment of the vowels as productive, distinct features and the contestants' treatment of them as tied to the lexicon is an example of structural elision. That is, while the n-th order productive California vowel phonology is taken up and stylized at the $n + 1$st order in the film, the contestants' $n + 2$nd order metastereotyping of the film characters elides this feature despite its presence in the original Bill and Ted stylization. This semiotic trajectory is of a taxonomically different type than that of *dude*, in which the lexical form is represented across all three indexical orders. Moreover, the $n + 2$nd order elision by Ricco and Munya may or may not be ideologically motivated. On the one hand, the elision may be deliberately used to simplify the style and foreground certain other salient features.

Figure 3. Bill and Ted's use of the 'air guitar' gesture

On the other hand, it may result from a nonnative orientation to American youth styles that lacks knowledge of these features.

Furthermore, speakers are less likely to be aware of the details of phonology than of larger, semantic signs (Silverstein 1981). For this reason, *dude* may be readily taken up by Ricco and Munya while the California vowel system is elided. However, other semantic symbols — both lexical and embodied — are frequently drawn on as part of the film's stylization but are nonetheless elided from the contestants' metastereotypic representation. At the lexical level, one such feature is among the most iconic constructions of the film: the *most* + modifier intensifier, exemplified by Ted's utterance from the film "You are going to have a most excellent adventure through history." At the level of embodied semiotics, another such symbol is an 'air guitar' gesture, in which Bill and Ted pretend to hold an imaginary guitar while strumming the strings. This gesture is overlaid with an electric guitar chord in the film's soundtrack, and it is used as an embodied positive evaluation of a preceding utterance as well as an index of the characters' identities as aspiring rock stars. Figure 3 shows the film characters performing this gesture.

Despite the prevalence of these forms in the film and references made by the contestants to "Bill and Ted's" membership in a band, neither the *most* + modifier nor the air guitar gesture are taken up by Ricco and Munya. In this way, these forms instantiate the same type of semiotic trajectory across indexical orders as California phonology, in which representations at the n-th and $n + 1$st orders are evident, but in which Ricco and Munya fail to further stylize the features at the $n + 2$nd order. Again, it is unclear whether the absence of these two forms is due to deliberate ideological erasure or lack of stylistic knowledge.

3.3 *N* + 1st and *n* + 2nd order representations only

While the semiotic trajectories examined so far project back to an *n*-th order California source style, one feature in particular is saliently represented at both the *n* + 1st order and then subsequently at the *n* + 2nd order, yet it is clearly not intended to project an *n*-th order source. Specifically, in the film, Bill and Ted frequently engage in simultaneous and coordinated speech and gesture. At the embodied level, this feature can be observed in the characters' co-production of the air guitar gesture in Figure 3 above. Example 5 shows this phenomenon of simultaneity at the linguistic level. Here, Bill and Ted have traveled to a castle in medieval Europe, where their unwelcome presence has just been discovered by the castle's king:

Example 5. *Bill and Ted's Excellent Adventure*
1   KING;   Put them in the Iron Maiden.
2   BILL;   [Iron Maiden? Excellent].
3   TED;   [Iron Maiden? Excellent].
4   KING;   Execute them!
5   BILL;   [Bogus].
6   TED;   [Bogus].

This discursive structure, demonstrated in lines 2 and 3 and in lines 5 and 6, is again facilitated by the scripted nature of the film genre and thus is unlikely to be a feature indexical of 'real' California style. However, the lack of an *n*-th order does not stop Ricco and Munya from attempting to stylize this feature:

Example 6. *Spoofing Bill and Ted*
45   MUNYA;   Let's like take, .. let's like, start a business, man,
46   RICCO;   ... I go for that too, ma:n,
47   [To]tally: <[todəli]> yeah: @:@: Awe:so[$_2$:me] [$_3$Awe:so:me Y][$_4$ea:h],
48   MUNYA;   [Like] —   [$_2$Awe:]so[$_3$:me:]   [$_4$Yea:h].

Although the spontaneous nature of the contestants' talk complicates the task of simultaneously exclaiming *awesome* and *yeah* on lines 47 and 48, it is clear that this is what they are attempting to do. Furthermore, their stylization of a feature that obviously does not source from *n*-th order everyday speech suggests that their explicit semiotic target is indeed a metastereotypic one (Bill and Ted) rather than a stereotypic one (the original California source style).

As I have demonstrated in this section, the semiotic trajectories of the features stylized in the film are not uniform in kind. On the one hand, features like *dude* are first stylized by Bill and Ted in the film at the *n* + 1st indexical order as stereotypic of *n*-th order California identities. *Dude* is then taken up and further hyperbolized at the *n* + 2nd order in the reality show — especially by Munya — as metastereotypic of Bill and Ted. On the other hand, other features stylized in the film are instantiated in semiotic trajectories through which these forms are not represented at either the *n*-th or *n* + 1st orders. Forms like productively stylized vowels, the air guitar gesture, and the *most* + modifier construction are elided by the contestants from the *n* + 2nd order despite their salience in the film as *n* + 1st order stylized features. Conversely, simultaneously coordinated speech and gesture — though hyperbolized by Bill and Ted and then further hyperbolized by Ricco and Munya — does not originally source from an *n*-th order representation. This taxonomic diversity of trajectories results from different ideological under-standings of features' links to styles held by performers across and within different indexical orders. These myriad trajectories are schematized in Figure 4.

Indexical Order	*n*-th	*n* + 1st	*n* + 2nd
Source	California youth	*Excellent Adventure* Film	*Big Brother* reality show
dude	yes	yes	yes
Calif. vowel phonology	yes	yes	*no*
most + modifier	yes	yes	*no*
air guitar gesture	yes	yes	*no*
simult. speech/gesture	*no*	yes	yes

Figure 4. Semiotic trajectories across indexical orders of stylized features from *Bill and Ted's Excellent Adventure*

4. Broader stylistic ideologies: *N* + 2nd order features sourced from beyond the film

In the previous section, I examined the diverse stylized features whose various semiotic trajectories all intersect at the *n* + 1st order. In this section, I focus instead on features that are taken up and stylized at the *n* + 2nd order by Ricco and Munya as part of their performance of Bill and Ted yet are absent or not salient in the original *n* + 1st order representation in the film. The speech chain networks link-ing the *n* + 2nd order representations of these features to the source styles from which they derive stretch back to the broader dude persona, California youth, or more general American youth cultural forms. The various stylistic associations of these features are exploited differently by Ricco and Munya in their stylizations of Bill and Ted. Ultimately, their use reveals the contestants' different ideological ori-entations regarding what constitutes congruence with the Bill and Ted target style.

The most frequent feature of this type in Ricco and Munya's performance — second only to *dude* in its prevalence — is *totally*. Like *dude*, *totally* appears in dense clusters, as illustrated in Example 7:

Example 7. *Spoofing Bill and Ted*

19	MUNYA;	Dude, you need to stop saying [that wor:d, ma:n].
20	RICCO;	[###]
21		… What wor::d, ma::n,
22	MUNYA;	… like, totally <[tərəli]>,
23	RICCO;	OK, totally <[todəli]> coo:l, I'll totally <[todli]> stop.
24	MUNYA;	… Totally <[tərəli]>.

In line 19, Munya makes a complaint about Ricco's frequent use of *totally*. Ironically and no doubt deliberately, Ricco's acquiescence in line 23 includes two additional tokens of the offending word. Here, the use of *totally* reveals an ideologically essential link between iconic feature and style: any effort by Ricco to thwart his own use of *totally* is represented by him as fruitless. Not to be outdone, Munya comes back on line 24 with an equally ironic token of *totally* himself; even after complaining about Ricco's use of this form, he portrays his character as being equally unable to eliminate *totally* from his own speech.

Ricco's use of *totally* is indeed heavy: he uses this form 22 times out of 795 total words while Munya uses it 20 times out of 895 total words. That is, Ricco utters *totally* on average once every 36 words while Munya utters it once every 47 words. For Ricco, then, *totally* is a much more ideologically salient resource for indexing the performed style than is *dude*. And although Munya uses *dude* more often than *totally*, his frequent use of the latter form is nonetheless ideologically salient. But while *dude* is frequently stylized both by the characters in *Excellent Adventure* and the reality show contestants alike, *totally* is not a stereotypic index in the film; the film characters on occasion do utter *totally*, but it is never performed in a hyperbolic fashion. Nevertheless, the contestants' exaggerated use of *totally* is not incongruent with the broader style common across all three indexical orders and shared with *dude*: perceptual dialectology studies have revealed language ideologies associating *totally* with Californians (Fought 2002), and more specifically, Southern Californians (Bucholtz et al. 2007). Ricco and Munya's uptake of *totally* thus appears to orient to this broader ideological vein. On the other hand, the relative absence of *totally* in the film compared to *dude* may be related to the fact that the iconic status of *totally* as an index of male California youth is a more recent phenomenon. That Ricco and Munya nonetheless stylize this form may have to do with the fact that, in order for them, in 2008, to hit the target of youthful, cutting-edge California dudes — part of the ideological essence of Bill and Ted —

they have to semiotically miss the target of the characters as they were originally performed, due to the time gap of 18 years.

This particular conflict between the temporality of language ideologies and semiotic faithfulness to the film is also reflected in hyperbolic n + 2nd order use of *like*, a form which, like *totally*, only rarely appears in the film. While Ricco does utter *like* a handful of times, it is again Munya who hyperbolizes this form. Although this form has been iconic of California for some time, in the past it has been ideologically associated more with the feminine "Valley Girl" persona (Dailey-O'Cain 2000; D'Arcy 2007). The more contemporary, gender-neutral ideology of *like* as an icon of California style offers it as another form through which Munya can display faithfulness to the ideology of the trendy youth style of Bill and Ted while semiotically diverging from the film's original bundling of stylistic features. Such stylization of *like* is demonstrated in Example 8, in which Munya and Ricco discuss the provider of the 'marijuana' (again, actually cigarettes) that they are smoking — a man whom Ricco, in jest, says he knows as "Big Brother" (i.e., the producer of the reality show):[6]

Example 8. *Spoofing Bill and Ted*
40   MUNYA;   Dude <[dɨd]>, he must totally <[tourəli]>, like, .. sell this, but like, I
41   mean like, .. on like a, on like, a global scale? You know <[nə]>,
42   [like] –
43   RICCO;   [duːde <[dɨd]>],
44   MUNYA;   Let's like take, .. let's like, start a business, man.

Ultimately, the use of *totally* and *like* by Munya, and to an overall lesser degree by Ricco, in stylizing two characters who rarely used these forms means that the contestants possess an ideological understanding of some broader style that semiotically subsumes both Bill and Ted and *totally* and *like*. In other words, Ricco and Munya are not just replicating stylistically decontextualized analogs of Bill and Ted. Rather, they are actively shaping stylistic representations by drawing on repertoires of features deriving from different sources that for them exhibit ideological congruence.

This phenomenon is especially evident in Ricco's lexical stylization of Bill and Ted, which includes forms such as *aight* (from *alright*), *bogus* (perhaps a tip of the hat to the film's sequel, *Bill and Ted's Bogus Journey* [1991]), *dog, nigga, phattest*, and *'na mean* (from *you know what I mean* [Reyes 2005]). Crucially, with the exception of *bogus*, these forms are sourced from beyond the film and index African American English (AAE) in general and a Hip Hop identity in particular.

---

6. The practice of smoking marijuana is an example of an embodied index of the dude persona stylized by Ricco and Munya yet not sourced from the film.

By contrast, Munya's heavy use of *dude*, *like*, and a smattering of other forms mostly not found in the film, such as *bro*, *sweet*, *awesome*, *off the hook*, and *wicked*, more closely indexes an ideologically white California youth style such as the dude persona (although *wicked* and *off the hook* may actually index Boston and AAE, respectively). Their use of these divergent features demonstrates Ricco and Munya to be positioning Bill and Ted in relation to their own ideological understandings of California and American youth cultural styles. Ricco's use of stylistically diverse features in performing Bill and Ted — from the dude persona to AAE — suggests that he is orienting to a broader language ideology that groups together various semiotic forms under the rubric of 'American youth culture.' In contrast, Munya's stylization points to a language ideology that is more tightly associated with the target style in the film.

However, simply stating that Munya's representation is more accurate than Ricco's would distort the relative ideological perspectives of both speaker and audience in which style resides. While Munya's performance might seem to certain American audiences more truly to represent California style, the fact that the responses to the clips posted by viewers on the *Big Brother Africa* website failed to make an evaluative distinction between the two contestants' performances is telling. That is, there is a lack of evidence that the majority African audience's ideological understanding of the style being performed is specifically oriented to Bill and Ted or California. In fact, viewer responses indicate a considerable amount of confusion as to the stylistic target of Ricco and Munya's parody. Thus, in such a loosely constrained ideological context for the performance of style, there is not a local basis for understanding Ricco's performance as 'less accurate.'

Ricco and Munya stylize a number of linguistic forms at the $n + 2$nd order that lack an $n + 1$st order representation in the film. These features vary in how closely they index the dude persona, with Ricco tending to draw on features from broader American youth identities (such as Hip Hop style) more than does Munya. Nevertheless, their use of these features from beyond the film demonstrates their own ideological understandings both of Bill and Ted's place within mediatized American youth styles and of what constitutes semiotic congruence with the styles that they are performing. Moreover, because the contestants' stylization is framed as a performance of these film characters, the features enlisted in this depiction project Bill and Ted as their original authors, regardless of whether the contestants sourced such features from the film or from elsewhere. Hence, the process of metastereotyping involves semiotic trajectories much more complicated than those that simply stretch back to the indexical order of the prior representation. As new audiences take up features for new stylizations, these trajectories incorporate forms both from within and beyond the broader dude persona, California, and American youth styles.

5.   The ideological evaluation of the dude persona

The analysis thus far has focused on how the performers' ideological understandings of styles are revealed through the features that they selectively hyperbolize and elide in their respective stereotypic and metastereotypic portrayals of California youth and Bill and Ted. But as previous work on mock language has demonstrated, the use of stylizations can also naturalize representations of particular groups' linguistic practices and (lack of) intelligence. In this section, I analyze how Ricco and Munya weave together explicit and implicit references to their characters' lack of intelligence with their use of semiotic practices discussed above. I show how, through these discourse strategies, the contestants forge an essential relation between style and lack of intelligence, and how this relation connects with globally circulating beliefs about American youth.

Example 7 in the previous section illustrates this discursive phenomenon: Ricco's performed obliviousness to his use of *totally* twice in the very act of agreeing not to use this form establishes an indexical association between his essential use of *totally* and the reason for this obliviousness — his lack of intelligence. That is, the use of the form ideologically invokes the social meaning. But it is throughout the aptly titled clip *Dumb and Dumber* that the issue of Bill and Ted's intellectual inadequacy becomes the central interactional topic. Here, the two try to 'out-dumb' each other in an effort to woo Hazel. Eventually, they resign themselves to the idea that they are just too smart, as seen in Example 2 above where Munya says, "when she says dumb, she means like, the opposite of us." Munya's ironically misperceived self assessment is further epitomized when he claims to realize the kind of 'dumb guy' that Hazel is seeking:

Example 9. *Dumb and Dumber*
47   MUNYA;   I think I know the dumb guy she wants.
48   　　　　　(H) <VOICE OF MUNYA> Hello Hazel? my na:me is Munya?
49   　　　　　… (tsk) Um:, … I am from: Zimbabwe.
50   　　　　　That was so <[sө]> dumb, yeah <[ya]>?

In line 48, Munya suspends his performance of Bill and switches to his own voice, albeit a version stylized for formality and learnedness: he uses full form *hello* and non-contracted *my name is* (line 48) and *I am* (line 49). Nonetheless, his introduction of himself must be understood as the 'dumb guy' promised by 'Bill' in the previous line. This introduction is closed off by line 50 by Munya's return to voicing Bill, marked by fronting of the vowel in *so,* centralization of the vowel in *yeah,* and the use of the informal tag *yeah* instead of *yes.* Thus, the voice of Munya is explicitly framed as dumb and that of Bill is implicitly framed as smart. But the widely established representations of learnedness and formality engendered by Munya's self-stylization subvert this explicit reading and point to an antithetical, ironic one: that Munya from Zimbabwe is actually the smart one and the stylized Bill persona is the dumb one. Furthermore, the features used to constitute Bill's voice become ideologically tied to this social meaning by virtue of their opposition to the learnedness and implied intelligence of Munya's own voice.

In the above opposition, the mention of Zimbabwe ideologically enters in on the side of high social value. This reference is not the only place in which Africanity is positioned in contrast to the American film characters' stupidity. In Example 12, Ricco, as Ted, asks Munya where Africa is located, following the latter's mention that the continent needs better marijuana:

Example 10. *Spoofing Bill and Ted*
56 RICCO;   Africa?
57 MUNYA;   Ye:ah.
58 RICCO;   That's in Europe, right?
59 MUNYA;   … Yeah, dude <[did]>? .. [Didn't you know that]?
60 RICCO;   [Oh:] oo:. [₂coo:l].
61 MUNYA;   [₂Africa's] like, .. this place in like,
62   .. the south of Europe?

Munya again draws on irony; it is silly that 'Ted' does not 'know' that Africa is in Europe. But this irony extends much farther, given the location of the show and the majority-African composition of its viewership. Thus, this same obviousness has a real-world instantiation: for all involved, it goes without saying where Africa is, and for Americans not to know this fact is silly. In this way, the contestants invoke a well-known stereotype of Americans' geographic ignorance. And like the other examples, displayed stupidity is juxtaposed with a stylized form with which it enters into an essential relationship: Munya's use of *dude* on line 59.

The example more broadly demonstrates how meanings created in and for one context (California and American youth) are transported by global entertainment networks to other parts of the world, where they are reinterpreted in relation to local meanings for local consumption. This hybridity has been of recent interest in discussions of other contemporary media forms, such as the glocalization of Hip Hop language practices across different transnational urban spaces (Alim 2009). In such cases, social actors in spaces traditionally peripheral to the global political economy are increasingly able, through participation in these new genres of media that foreground unscripted, 'real' voices, to agentively reinterpret and produce on a global scale. In reality television, for example, 'real' people are mediatized, and their voices are circulated not only back to the population from which they originate, but also to the rest of the world through the Internet and satellite television. In this way, stylized reinterpretations of hegemonic styles become a way of talking back to the West. Moreover, as such Internet access and satellite television become prioritized luxury items even among those with limited disposable incomes, these voices are gaining wider reach in Africa.

But with this new mediatization of unscripted talk, the speakers are increasingly beholden to the contingencies of having a broad audience: alongside the necessity of highlighting prior authorship, such stylizations need to draw on widely circulating ideologies to achieve semiotic recognizability. To be sure, the confused viewer responses that failed to distinguish between Ricco and Munya's stylization points to this fact. As higher and higher indexical orders of stylization land geographically farther and farther from the stylistic source, the ideological access of the audience to the original style tends to taper off, reducing both stylistic recognizability and performer accountability. However, with the continued growth of both local audiences and glocalizing intertextualities in these new forms of media, new ideological understandings of globalized style are sure to spread. In this rapidly changing ideological terrain, the analysis of the trajectories of speech chain networks across transnational spaces provides a crucial mapping of the global transformations of the social domains of enregistered features.

6. Conclusion

In this paper, I have investigated how mediatized performances that parody 'real' speech styles get reinterpreted through further acts of mediatized stylizations. In this $n + 2$nd order reinterpretation, the prior $n + 1$st order stereotyping of the original n-th target style is reproduced. I have termed this discursive phenomenon metastereotyping, and I have described the multiplex semiotic trajectories of the features that performers use when enacting a metastereotypic performance. As each successive representation is taken up and further stylized by subsequent social actors, prior features are hyperbolized and elided, while new features are brought in from beyond the scope of the prior representation(s), or even from beyond the broader target style. These features from beyond the prior representation are bundled together with those from within it, and they thus reveal the performers' wider understandings of the styles of which the parodied personas are only one part. Furthermore, the metastereotypic representation is a site not only for portraying a group as speaking in a particular way, but also for demonstrating how this way of speaking ideologically reflects inherent qualities about the group, such as a lack of intelligence. Taken together, the semiotic and ideological dimensions of metastereotypic stylizations analyzed here expose globally circulating stereotypes about a particular type of Californian and more broadly American youth style.

References

Agha, Asif. 2007. Language and Social Relations [Studies in the Social and Cultural Foundation of Language 24]. Cambridge: Cambridge University Press.

Alim, H. Samy. 2009. Straight Outta Compton, Straight *aus München*: Global Linguistic Flows, Identities, and the Politics of Language in a Global Hip Hop Nation. In: Global Linguistic Flows: Hip Hop Cultures, Youth Identities, and the Politics of Language, H. Samy Alim, Awad Ibrahim, and Alastair Pennycook (eds.), 1–22. New York: Routledge.

Appadurai, Arjun. 1990. Disjuncture and Difference in the Global Cultural Economy. Theory, Culture, and Society 7, 295–310.

Auer, Peter. 2007. Style and Social Identities: Alternative Approaches to Linguistic Heterogeneity [Language, Power, and Social Process 18]. New York: Mouton de Gruyter.

Bucholtz, Mary. 2010. White Kids: Language, Race, and Styles of Youth Identity. Cambridge: Cambridge University Press.

Bucholtz, Mary, Nancy Bermudez, Victor Fung, Lisa Edward, and Rosalva Vargas. 2007. Hella Nor Cal or Totally So Cal?: The Perceptual Dialectology of California. Journal of English Linguistics 35, 4, 325–352.

Chun, Elaine. 2004. Ideologies of Legitimate Mockery: Margaret Cho's Revoicings of Mock Asian. Pragmatics 14, 2/3, 263–289.

Coupland, Nikolas. 2007. Style: Language Variation and Identity [Key Topics in Sociolinguistics]. Cambridge: Cambridge University Press.

Dailey-O'Cain, Jennifer. 2000. The Sociolinguistic Distribution of and Attitudes toward Focuser *like* and Quotative *like*. Journal of Sociolinguistics 4, 1, 60–80.

D'Arcy, Alexandra. 2007. *Like* and Language Ideology: Disentangling Fact from Fiction. American Speech 82, 4, 386–419.

Du Bois, John W. 2007. The Stance Triangle. In: Stancetaking in Discourse: Subjectivity, Evaluation, Interaction, Robert Englebretson (ed), 139–182 [Pragmatics & Beyond New Series 164]. Amsterdam: John Benjamins.

Du Bois, John W., Susanna Cumming, Stephan Schuetze-Coburn, Danae Paolino. 1992. Discourse Transcription [Santa Barbara Papers in Linguistics 4]. Santa Barbara, Calif.: University of California, Santa Barbara Department of Linguistics.

Eckert, Penelope. 2004. The Meaning of Style. Presentation, Eleventh Annual Symposium About Language and Society — Austin (SALSA). Austin: Department of Linguistics, The University of Texas.

Eckert, Penelope. California Vowels. <http://www.stanford.edu/~eckert/vowels.html>. Accessed 22 May 2010.

Fought, Carmen. 2002. California Students' Perceptions of, You Know, Regions and Dialects? In: Handbook of Perceptual Dialectology, volume 2, Daniel Long and Dennis R. Preston (eds), 177–136. Amsterdam: John Benjamins.

Hill, Jane H. 1993. Is it Really "No Problemo?" Presentation, Junk Spanish and Anglo-Racism. First Annual Symposium About Language and Society — Austin (SALSA). Austin: Department of Linguistics, The University of Texas.

Hill, Jane H. 2008. The Everyday Language of White Racism [Blackwell Studies in Discourse and Culture]. Malden, Mass.: Wiley-Blackwell.

Hinton, Leanne, Birch Moonwomon, Sue Bremner, Herb Luthin, Mary Van Clay, Jean Lerner, and Hazel Corcoran. 1987. It's Not Just the Valley Girls: A Study of California English.

In: Proceedings of the Thirteenth Annual Meeting of the Berkeley Linguistics Society, Jon Aske, Natasha Beery, Laura Michaelis, and Hana Filip (eds), 117–128. Berkeley, Calif.: Berkeley Linguistics Society.

Irvine, Judith. 2001. Style as Distinctiveness: The Culture and Ideology of Linguistic Differentiation. In: Style and Sociolinguistic Variation, Penelope Eckert and John Rickford (eds), 21–43. Cambridge: Cambridge University Press.

Irvine, Judith and Susan Gal. 2000. Language Ideology and Linguistic Differentiation. In: Regimes of Language, Paul Kroskrity (ed), 35–83 [Advanced Seminar Series]. Santa Fe, New Mex.: School of American Research Press.

Johnstone, Barbara, Jennifer Andrus, and Andrew E. Danielson. 2006. Mobility, Indexicality, and the Enregisterment of Pittsburghese. Journal of English Linguistics 34, 2, 77–104.

Kiesling, Scott. 2004. Dude. American Speech 79, 3, 281–305.

Labrador, Roderick N. 2004. "We Can Laugh at Ourselves": Hawai'i Ethnic Humor, Local Identity and the Myth of Multiculturalism. Pragmatics 14, 2/3, 291–316.

Lundquist, Lynne L. 1996. Myth and Illiteracy: Bill and Ted's Explicated Adventures. Extrapolation: A Journal of Science Fiction and Fantasy 37, 3, 212–223.

Meek, Barbra A. 2006. And the Injun Goes "How!": Representations of American Indian English in White Public Space. Language in Society 35, 93–128.

Mendoza-Denton, Norma. 2008. Homegirls: Language and Cultural Practice among Latina Youth Gangs [New Directions in Ethnography 2]. Malden, Mass.: Wiley-Blackwell.

MultiChoice Reaches 2 Million Subscribers. 29 November 2007. <http://mybroadband.co.za/news/Telecoms/2101.html>. Accessed July 15, 2010.

Rahman, Jacquelyn J. 2004. It's a Serious Business: The Linguistic Construction of Middle-Class White Characters by African American Narrative Comedians, [Unpublished Doctoral Dissertation]. Stanford University.

Reyes, Angela. 2005. Appropriation of African American Slang by Asian American Youth. Journal of Sociolinguistics 9, 4, 509–532.

Ronkin, Maggie, and Helen E. Karn. 1999. Mock Ebonics: Linguistic Racism in Parodies of Ebonics on the Internet. Journal of Sociolinguistics 3, 3, 360–380.

Roth-Gordon, Jennifer. 2009. Conversational Sampling, Race Trafficking, and the Invocation of the Gueto in Brazilian Hip Hop. In: Global Linguistic Flows: Hip Hop Cultures, Youth Identities, and the Politics of Language, H. Samy Alim, Awad Ibrahim, and Alastair Pennycook (eds), 63–77. New York: Routledge.

Shankar, Shalini. 2004. Reel to Real: Desi Teens' Linguistic Engagements with Bollywood. Pragmatics 14, 2/3, 317–335.

Silverstein, Michael. 1981. The Limits of Awareness. Sociolinguistic Working Paper, 84. Austin: Southwest Educational Development Lab, 1–30.

Silverstein, Michael. 2003. Indexical Order and the Dialectics of Sociolinguistic Life. Language and Communication 23, 193–229.

Shary, Timothy. 1998. Reification and Loss in Postmodern Puberty: The Cultural Logic of Fredric Jameson and American Youth Movies. In: Postmodernism in the Cinema, Cristina Degli-Esposti (ed), 73–89. New York: Berghahn Books.

Spitulnik, Debra. 1997. The Social Circulation of Media Discourse and the Mediation of Communities. Journal of Linguistic Anthropology 6, 2, 161–187.

Troyer, John, and Chani Marchiselli. 2005. Slack, Slacker, Slackest: Homosocial Bonding Practices in Contemporary Dude Cinema. In: Where the Boys Are: Cinemas of Masculinity and Youth, Murray Pomerance and Frances Gateward (eds), 264–276. Detroit: Wayne State University Press.

Urban, Greg. 1991. A Discourse-Centered Approach to Culture. Austin: University of Texas Press.

Appendix. Transcription Conventions

<[ ]>	phonetic transcription of immediately prior word
< >	particular manner of stylized speech
</ >	end of particular manner of stylized speech
..	short pause
…	long pause
,	continuing intonation
.	terminal intonation
?	rising intonation
=	latched utterances
#	uncertain transcription
:	prosodic lengthening
[]	overlap
[₂]	second overlap, etc.
@	laughter
(( ))	contextual and gestural information
-	truncated word
—	truncated intonation unit

Anime and intertextualities
Hegemonic identities in *Cowboy Bebop*

Mie Hiramoto
National University of Singapore

Cowboy Bebop, a popular anime series set in the year 2071 onboard the space-ship *Bebop*, chronicles the bohemian adventures of a group of bounty hunters. This paper presents how the imaginary characters and their voices are conventionalized to fit hegemonic norms. The social semiotic of desire depicted in *Cowboy Bebop* caters to a general heterosexual market in which hero and babe characters represent the anime archetypes of heterosexual normativity. Scripted speech used in the anime functions as a role language which indexes common ideological attributes associated with a character's demeanor. This study focuses on how ideas, including heterosexual normativity and culture-specific practices, are reproduced in media texts in order to negotiate the intertextual distances that link the characters and audience.

1. Introduction: Media intertextuality

Modernity has seen a widespread implementation of the institutionalization of standard language and discourse, although in reality varieties of language and discourse are able to coexist, if in a somewhat disorderly manner. In Foucault's (1980) terms, the semiotic construction of discourse practices depends on general rules that characterize the discursive formation to which they belong. The semiotic notion of intertextuality introduced by Kristeva (1980) refers to connections between a text and other previous or synchronic texts across time and space. When characters are created in media, discourse practices are strategically assigned to such characters in order to assign them to their given roles (see Lazar and Wahl this issue) by utilizing existing concepts and conventions. Thus, even the creation of a new personality is not entirely new as its attributes are constructed through intertextual discursive practices based on preexisting social norms.

Park (2009: 548) states that media is one of the most influential of the institutions that connect disparate groups into an imagined community (Anderson

1983). When imaginary characters are created, their language use reflects the social ideologies that the creators wish to use or convey. Also, the creators may take a variety of stances toward these social/linguistic hierarchies and expectations. Gal and Irvine (1995) and Gal (1998) discuss the construction of ideologies through the semiotic processes of iconization and erasure (also see Wee 2006). Iconization refers to the idea that "linguistic differences that index social contrasts are reinterpreted as *icons* of the social contrasts" such that "the ideological representation fuses some quality of the linguistic feature and a supposedly parallel quality of the social group and understands one as the cause or the inherent, essential, explanation of the other" (Gal 1998: 328, italics in original). Gal (1995) also notes how language relates to power by pointing out the fact that certain linguistic variants are more highly valued than others in a culture. Simultaneously, resistance to the dominant culture occurs in linguistic practices and some people purposely choose to use devalued linguistic variants. "These devalued practices often propose or embody alternate models of the social world" (Gal 1995: 175) and both valued and devalued linguistic variants become sources of social power. Ideologies may be iconized or involve iconization; moreover, they may also be the vehicles of indexical relations between language and the social. Hill's (2005: 114) discussion of Mock Spanish exemplifies this concept of iconization. She states that Mock Spanish entails inferences that are a reduction and production of negative racist stereotypes of Spanish speakers, and that its use implicates all members of historically Spanish-speaking people to be

> lazy, dirty, unintelligent, sexually loose, and politically corrupt, as persons who speak a language that is not only disorderly and somewhat primitive but also easy and well suited to insincerity, and talk suited to sloth, filth, licentiousness, and the like (Hill 2005: 114).

The notion of erasure refers to a process "in which ideology, in simplifying the field of linguistic practices, renders some persons or activities or sociolinguistic phenomena invisible" (Gal and Irvine 1995: 974). Within Japanese society, Standard Japanese (SJ) is widely recognized as a special register of linguistic resource. In the media, it is socially expected of and thus assigned to a limited group of people who are considered to be stereotypically normative Japanese people. The SJ linguistic ideology endows speakers of this register with sophisticated qualities, at least superficially in regimented, or centralized, media discourse. Examining Japanese women's language (JWL) in SJ, Inoue (2003) writes that certain linguistic resources such as sentence final particles including *wa, wayo, noyo, dawa,* and *kashira,* mark softness, uncertainty, and other 'weak' affects which project normative femininity. These particles function as markers of normative femaleness when used by Japanese speakers; therefore, the particles function as "the socially-accepted and culturally-constituted gendered demeanor" in Japanese (Inoue 2003:319). Her argument is based on Ochs's notion of indexicality as summarized in Table 1:

Table 1. Indexing gender in Japanese, adopted from Ochs (1992:342)

Linguistic form	Direct index	Indirect index
ze, zo, daze, dana, kayo, etc.	coarse intensity	male 'voice'
wa, wayo, noyo, none, kashira, etc.	delicate intensity	female 'voice'

Inoue (2003) investigates the use of JWL and SJ in the novel *Sekiryô Kôya* 'Solitude Point' written by Yoshimeki in 1993. The female protagonist of the story, a 64-year-old Japanese woman named Yukie, is supposedly from a non-SJ speaking region in western Japan and grew up in a working class family. However, in the story, not only does she speak flawless SJ but she also uses prototypical JWL including the particles shown in Table 1 above. Realistically, it is highly unlikely that a woman of Yukie's background would speak either SJ or JWL. Her speech style thus demonstrates the aforementioned process of erasure, as it "reasserts the unity and homogeneity of Japanese language and, thereby, that of women's language" (Inoue 2003:325) by overshadowing Yukie's real identity as an uneducated regional-dialect-speaker from a rural area.

As explained by Eckert and McConnell-Ginet (2003), the success of a dominant ideology depends on its ability to convince people that it is not a matter of ideology, but simply natural, the way things are (Eckert and McConnell-Ginet 2003:43). They refer to this process as naturalization, the construction of a social norm based on the general consensus of what needs no explanation because people believe it is how things are: baby gift colors should be pink for girls and blue for boys, uneducated people should speak with a Tôhoku accent while educated city-dwellers should speak SJ. Naturalization means more or less the same thing as the idea of iconization discussed above. This paper aims to investigate iconization/naturalization as concerns both normative and non-normative characters in the popular anime, *Cowboy Bebop* (*CB*), which won the approval of international viewers, by investigating correlations between the type of language used and the normative/non-normative traits associated with the characters in the show. The results of the study suggest that the crucial role of scripted speech in *CB* is to construct a language ideology that is far from a realistic portrayal of the speech of everyday practitioners of language. Consider Agha's (2005:38) discussion of enregisterment, the "processes whereby distinct forms of speech come to be socially recognized (or enregistered) as indexical of speaker attributes by a population of language users." The media employ such enregisterment as a method for simplifying complicated discursive practice. It is quite common for Japanese media discourse practice to not make use of the realities of the distribution of both regional and social Japanese dialects, e.g. representing characters that in real life would speak in a regional or social dialect, with a standard variety. Media characters that belong to certain subgroups are bound by specific sociolinguistic expectations (e.g. according to age, gender, socioeconomic status, regional affiliation, personal traits) to project stereotypical roles that they are assigned to. Thus, institutions such as media promote simplified interactions typified by linguistic enregisterment, thereby reproducing language and power relationships through intertextual discursive practices (Agha 2005). An example of the regimentation of language concerning imaginary speakers of Japanese can be seen in Kinsui's (2003, 2007) work on 'role language.' He lists linguistic features used by imaginary characters in novels, dramas, anime, translations, etc., and calls them *yakuwarigo* 'role language.' This assignment of linguistic registers is based on the semiotic process of iconization and erasure, as it helps audiences identify stereotypical images related to imaginary characters' roles. Yukie from *Sekiryô Kôya* in Inoue's (2003) analysis, mentioned earlier, provides an example: her countryside working class family origins have been erased by JWL, as her given identity in the novel was a stereotypical 'Japanese woman' in her senior years. Yukie gets jealous because people label her as 'a war bride' whereas her daughter-in-law is depicted as 'a bride of an international marriage.' Even in the situations where Yukie reveals her jealousy of her young, educated, city-born daughter-in-law, Yukie's introspections are in JWL, her 'role language' in the story. *Yakuwarigo* is a facet of the regimentation of the Japanese language which correlates specific linguistic registers' pragmatic and semantic meanings with characters that embody expected roles. Kinsui (2003) also claims that SJ is usually reserved for protagonists while some social or regional dialects (or even pseudo dialects) are used by side characters with specific attributes. For example, the Ôsaka dialect is assigned to money-oriented, funny characters, while the Tôhoku dialect is for uneducated, unsophisticated characters; similarly, American Southern slave characters in translations of novels such as *Gone with the Wind* or *Uncle Tom's Cabin* speak a pseudo dialect that resembles the use of Tôhoku dialect in the Japanese context (see Gaubatz 2007; Hiramoto 2009). Similarly, Lippi-Green's (1997) work shows how accents and dialects are associated with fictional characters in media, suggesting that these language propagations promote the inequalities between the mainstream and socially subordinate languages.

A number of researchers have reported on issues of language, gender, and sexuality and their link to issues of power and ideology. This study also observes the ways in which a medium of Japanese pop culture like anime constructs hegemonic heterosexuality (as well as hegemonic masculinity), and the ways in which these are made identifiable to the audience. Kiesling (e.g. 2002/2006, 2005) investigates how a group of fraternity house members at a North American university emphasizes heterosexual male dominance, while female and homosexual male subordination is highlighted by the members' construction of gender ideologies via language use. He demonstrates "how language is used by the men to reproduce a hegemonic heterosexuality which is embedded in the larger context of hegemonic masculinity" (Kiesling 2002/2006: 129). The examples include the members' use of address terms toward other males, and their stories of drinking and their sexual exploits with women. These data demonstrate constructions and reproductions of heterosexual male dominance by the members in order to claim power in a same-sex social group. He also notes:

> What we see here is that heterosexual identities and ideologies are being created in a much more complex way: there is really no separated group of heterosexuals in the dominant culture. This group, like men a few decades ago, is considered the norm, and is indeed hardly a coherent group. But we have seen here that we can identify heterosexuality as part of these men's socially constructed identity.
>
> (Kiesling 2002/2006: 129)

The idea of hegemonic masculinity or normative sexuality is well reflected and represented in mainstream media discourse including scripted speech used in pop culture such as movies, comics, games, and anime. The ideas of a conventional popularity, the conventional ideas of what it means to be a popular person within a particular social group, support associations of normative males and females with the language of power, e.g. standard or gender-appropriate varieties (Lippi-Green 1997). The linguistic conformity associated with the normative ideology of gender and sexuality is easily attainable through performance if one wishes to show compliance with the hegemonic hetero-normative ideology (e.g. Hall 1995) and this is straightforwardly done in media discourse. As pointed out by Inoue (2003), highly idealized JWL has became the property of imagined characters like Minnie Mouse or Barbie, while hardly any Japanese women would speak in that way in reality. Likewise, in what follows I will demonstrate how idealized language is assigned to fictional characters in the anime in order to appeal to a specific semiotics of desire that is assumed to be the norm of today's society.

2.   Data and methodology

CB, originally released in Japan in 1998, was used as data for this study. Susan Napier, the author of *Anime from Akira to Howl's Moving Castle: Experiencing Contemporary Japanese Animation*, writes, "[CB] gained an intense following both in America and Japan precisely because it took certain conventions of masculinity and explored them on a deep and emotionally satisfying level" (Napier 2005: xiii).

The story is set largely on the futuristic spaceship *Bebop* in the year 2071, and follows the adventures of a group of bounty hunters (two male and two female): ex-triad member Spike Spiegel, ex-cop Jet Black, sexy con-artist Faye Valentine, and child computer hacker Radical Edward. The show became extremely successful internationally and remains one of the most popular anime outside Japan today. The anime movie version was released in 2003 and a live action version is in production in Hollywood. *CB*'s target audience is young adults, not children. The show was selected for this study because of its stereotypical portrayal of hegemonic ideology based on heterosexual norms represented in a "social semiotic of desire" as explained by Cameron and Kulick (2003: 140):

> [I]t is important to acknowledge that desire is materialized and conveyed through semiotic resources that are variably distributed among members of the societies in which they are used. As Penelope Eckert (2002) has observed, there will be structured variation in people's use of what we have called the 'social semiotic of desire', because different kinds of people are socialized to desire different things, and/or to express their desires in different ways. (Cameron and Kulick 2003: 140)

The point here, however, is that the social semiotic of desire depicted in *CB* caters to a general heterosexual market. Hero and babe characters represent anime archetypes of heterosexual normativity, as, in Eckert and McConnell-Ginet's words (2003: 35), they are modeled after universally quintessential men and women: such as Superman and Scarlett O'Hara. The heterosexual norms in *CB* are established

Figure 1. Main male characters, Jet and Spike

Figure 2. Main female characters, Faye and Ed

through semiotic resources such as body image and language use. Images of the main characters of *CB* are shown in Figures 1 and 2.

Spike and Jet are both mentally and physically skilled, although both have prosthetic body parts due to previous battle injuries. Spike is a master of Bruce Lee's Jeet Kune Do and an excellent gunman while Jet is an experienced mechanic and capable programmer who loves bonsai gardening. Additionally, not only do Spike and Jet speak idealized, rough men's language throughout the series, including the masculine sentence final particles shown in Table 1, they are excellent fighters and extraordinary pilots. Faye's seemingly aggressive background as a bounty-hunter and a con-artist is conveyed quite clearly through her addiction to gambling and penchant for street fighting, but she also consciously maintains her beauty. In her work on *Sailor Moon* (Toei Animation 1992/2002, original by Naoko Takeuchi), Allison (2000: 269) reports that one of the fans she interviewed, a 9-year-old girl, said she likes *Sailor Moon* because the title character has a great figure (*sutairu ga ii*) and not because she is powerful. Allison (2000: 269) goes on to say that this is the reason why some older men like the show — the character is viewed as a 'sex icon' and is an example of the infantilized female sex object, the idolization of which has become a general trend in Japan (see also Cornog and Perper 2005). Faye from *CB* is also definitely objectified; a magazine reviewer describes her as "a standard anime cutie with perky grapefruit-shaped boobs and tiny pert mouth" (Maio 2003: 95) and says that he suspects teen boy viewers enjoy watching a particular segment where Faye is abducted and ends up bound and disheveled on the floor (Maio 2003:95). As the babe character, Faye generally shows strong JWL characteristics. These three main characters, as portrayed by the art work and their language, are aligned with hegemonic gender and linguistic ideology. However, the other female main character, Ed, remains an oddball throughout the series as her name, looks, and language use obscure her femininity.

For this study, all 26 episodes of *CB* were transcribed; each episode runs about 23 minutes. Stories are structured with largely self-contained plots, and feature different guest protagonists, side characters, and villains. The total data covers about 600 minutes of audiovisual recording, excluding opening and closing credits and previews. The American English translations used in this paper are based on the dubbing of the *CB*, not on the subtitles.

3. Masculine and feminine voices

Japanese is known to have gender exclusive expressions, and the features of JWL, including sentence final particles, pronouns, lexical items, and discourse styles have been studied extensively (e.g. Ide 1982; Reynolds 1985; Shibamoto 1985; Mc-Gloin 1990; Okamoto 1995). Regarding first person pronouns, *watashi* is considered gender-neutral, while *ore* and *boku* are masculine and *atashi* and *atakushi* are feminine; there are many other forms available depending on speakers' social status and age as well as the current conversational context. Within the gender-exclusive pronominal categories, different pronouns carry different connotations. Within the masculine category, *boku* is considered casual, *ore* is rough. Another first person pronoun, *washi*, can be interpreted in two different ways: as a marker of a provincial accent or of an elderly male authority's voice. In some regions (e.g. Hiroshima, Nagano, or Aichi prefectures), *washi* is used by both male and female speakers.

Table 2. First person pronouns

Masculine (Colloquial)			Neutral (Formal)		Feminine (Colloquial)	
Casual	Rough	Old	Formal	Neutral	Formal	Casual
boku	*ore*	*washi*	*watakushi*	*watashi*	*atakushi*	*atashi*

As mentioned, the normative main characters were assigned with expected normative SJ. The bounty hunter heroes sound like tough men and the sexy female sounds quite feminine. Normative guest characters were also assigned with SJ, and similarly spoke in a manner indicating their conformity to gendered speech norms. Example 1 demonstrates normative characters' male and female voices heard in guest protagonists' speech:

(1)   Rhint and Alisa, Episode 10: *Ganymede Elegy*
      After Alisa's boyfriend, Rhint, accidentally kills a loan shark who was after
      Alisa, they plan to run away together.
      Rhint: *Ore o saguri ni kitan da... Kusô, shôkin o kakerareteru noka... Mô
               dame da...! Mô dame da...!*
               He's after me... I have a bounty on my head... It's all over...!
      Alisa: *Anata wa warukunai wa... Atashi ga anna yatsu kara okane o karita
               kara... atashi o mamotte kuretan janai...*
               It's not your fault... It's because I borrowed money from a crook
               like him. I should've never let you get mixed up in this.
      Rhint: *Tsukamattara mô tasukaranê, ore wa koroshichimattan da ze...*
               If I get caught, nothing can save me... nothing. I killed him.
      Alisa: *Nigemashô... Nigeru noyo, futari de!*
               Let's go. We've gotta run, right now!

In the data, all the male characters in protagonist roles spoke normative SJ and
in a masculine way. This was true for Gren, a guest protagonist with a soft and
kindly demeanor, who is a gay saxophone player (Episodes 12 & 13: *Jupiter Jazz 1
& 2*). Gren, an openly gay character, has a mainstream male role and speaks as one
would expect a man to speak. In Example 2, Faye and Gren discuss his homosexu-
ality; Gren employs masculine speech and Faye, feminine, throughout.

(2)   Faye and Gren, Episode 12: *Jupiter Jazz 1*
      [at a bar]
      Faye: *Atashi wa mitame hodo karui onna janai wa.*
               I'm not as simple as I seem, Mr. Saxophone.
      Gren: *Ainiku onna niwa kyômi ga nakute...*
               Women aren't my style. Sorry.
      Faye: *Ara, zannen...*
               Oh, what a pity.
      [after deciding to go to Gren's house]
      Gren: *Kantan ni shinnyôshite î noka?*
               And you trust me, just like that.
      Faye: *Onna niwa kyômi nain desho?*
               You said you weren't interested in women.

The contrast between Gren's use of the masculine particle *noka*, and Faye's use of
feminine forms such as the pronoun *atashi* and the particle *wa* (with rising intonation) is obvious. In addition, she uses the sentence-initial filler, *ara*, as well as
the interrogative marker *desho* with a rising intonation, also feminine. Examples 1
and 2 demonstrate that the normative register is reserved for protagonists, as one
would expect from Kinsui's (2003: 51, 70–72) observations on role language.

On the other hand, side characters are often assigned with role languages which help to iconize certain non-normative or otherwise undesirable traits. Kinsui (2003: 173) points out that men categorized as *nyû hâfu* 'cross-dresser, literally *new half* or *okama* 'male homosexual' often speak JWL in Japanese media. In the data, the only male characters in the entire series who spoke women's language were a group of cross-dressers in Episode 12 (*Jupiter Jazz 1*). Unlike Gren, the guest protagonist, the cross-dressers, living on a womanless planet, were assigned *okama kotoba* 'JWL spoken by men,' sometimes known as *onê kotoba* 'big sisters' language.' Fushimi (1991: 21) notes that although the internalization of feminine language in *onê kotoba* is an extension of JWL, it is often realized as a grotesquely exaggerated parody (cited in Suzuki 1998: 81). In Example 3, Spike, in search of his estranged girlfriend Julia, ends up meeting a cross-dresser prostitute named Julius during his search.

(3)   Julius and Spike, Episode 12: *Jupiter Jazz 1*
      Julius: *Shitsurei ne! Juria janai <u>wa</u>, Ju-ri-a-su, Juriasu yo!*
                    Sorry sailor, I'm not Julia. Ju-li-US. My name's Julius.
      Spike: *A, so...*
                    My mistake.
      ...
      Julius: *A, sô da, Guren nara nanika shitteru kamo... Mae ni onna to isshodatta no, mitakoto aru <u>wa</u>.*
                    Y'know, Gren's really the one who might be able to help. I've seen him with women on occasion.
      J's friend: *Ara, okyaku?*
                    Oh, a customer?
      Julius: *Chigau <u>wayo</u>. Dômitemo nonke <u>desho</u>? Sa, basho kaemasho.*
                    'Fraid not, darling. Can't you see he's straight? C'mon. Let's try another corner.

In Example 3, Julius, in his *onê kotoba*, uses the feminine features *wa*, *wayo*, and *desho*. His cross-dresser friend employs the feminine sentence-initial filler *ara*. This non-normative language use indexes simplistic assumptions based on superficial interpretations of the characters' sexuality. In the last line, Julius refers to Spike as *nonke*, common jargon among homosexuals to refer to a straight person (Abe 2004: 208). This interaction serves to make explicit the fact that a straight male like Spike only desires a straight female and to reinforce Spike's heterosexuality. As the cross-dresser prostitutes live on a womanless planet, and considering the comments made by other, frustrated, heterosexual male characters who reside there (see Example 4 below), it is implied that the cross-dressers' clients are not necessarily all homosexual males. Julius's sexuality is never discussed and his rather complicated gender and sexual identities are simply classified as belonging in a 'non-normative' category; he is presented as the binary opposite of normative, woman-loving Spike.

(4) Comments by men on the womanless planet, Episodes 12 & 13: *Jupiter Jazz 1 & 2*

[on a street, a group of men following Faye]

MAN: *Ojôsan, sono kakkô wa me no doku da. Soretomo sasottenno kai?*
Madam, your appearance is harmful to the eyes. Or are you trying to entice us?

FAYE: *Nnn, sô nanoyo. Chotto mattete ne.*
Oops! You found me out! Just hold on a minute.

[at a bar, a bartender talking to Jet]

BARTENDER: *Â, namami no onna o mitanowa hantoshi buri, gokujô no onna tte kotode ieba ninen buri da. Mimachigaeruwake nai desho.*
Oh yeah… It's been six months since I saw a woman in the flesh and two years since I saw a girl that good-looking. Trust me, I wouldn't make a mistake about that!

JET: *Kono machi niwa sumitakanê na...*
Man, I sure wouldn't wanna live around here.

While Julius's term in Example 3, the gay term *nonke*, meaning 'a straight man,' highlights Spike's normative sexuality, it establishes Julius's own identity as an unambiguously non-straight sex-worker who caters to male clients who desire his superficially feminine appearance on the womanless planet. Through this, Spike's normativity and Julius's non-normativity are brought to the audience's attention.

Quite dissimilarly, Ed, the other main female character, hardly uses gendered expressions at all. Her name, as well as the other characters' repeated comments on the ambiguity of her gender, help to reinforce Ed's heterosexually non-normative identity.

(5) Comments on Ed's gender

Faye talking to Ed, Episode 9: *Jamming with Edward*

Faye: *Ara, anta, onna no ko nano?*
Hey, you're a girl?

A security guard suspecting Ed's gender, Episode 23: *Brain Scratch*

Guard: *Musumette...? Honto ni onnanoko ka?*
She's an unusual looking child. Is she a girl?

Ed's father meeting with Spike and Jet, Episode 24: *Hard Luck Woman*

Father: *Ô sô ka. Musuko ga sewan natta. N? Musume datta ka?*

> Oh, that's different. Thanks for taking care of my son... Or, uh, was it my daughter?

Ed, as seen in Example 5, is portrayed as decidedly gender-neutral or ambiguous. Her non-conformity to feminine norms is not depicted by the use of masculine features, but rather by her predominant use of neutral features. In other words, interestingly, the lack of feminine features (JWL), not the use of masculine features, helps to construct Ed's non-femininity, thus, adding masculine elements to her characteristics. Ed is categorized as [−feminine] (or androgynous) because of her [−JWL] condition, and not because of her use of masculine features.

4.   Standard and non-standard voices

There are several side characters in the data who speak regional dialects. Kinsui (2003) notes that certain regional dialects function as role language to assign stereotypical traits to imaginary characters: Ôsaka or generally Kansai dialect-speaking characters' in popular media such as manga, anime, and plays tend to be loquacious, funny, frugal, food-loving, unsophisticated, etc. (Kinsui 2003: 81–101). In one episode of *CB*, a male side character named Otto, a freight ship driver, speaks with Hiroshima dialect. Some grammatical characteristics of Hiroshima dialect are presented in the following table.

Table 3. Hiroshima dialect

Grammar	Hiroshima dialect	SJ
Copula	*-ja*	*-da*
Sentence final particle	*-no, -wa/-ya*	*-ne, -yo*
Modal 'must/ have to'	*-nyâ*	*-naito/-neba*
Modal 'to give' (derogatory)	*-yoru*	*-yagaru*

In Example 6, Otto speaks to a fellow pilot, a guest female protagonist, V.T., about his hit-and-run accident.

(6)   V.T. and Otto, Episode 7: *Heavy Metal Queen*
       V.T.:   *Ah, Ottô, dôshita no?*
               Hey, Otto. What's up?
       Otto: *Atenige saretan ja. ... Gêto no iriguchi de ikinari warikonde kite, butsukete ikiyotta. Kusô, benshô sasenyâ ki ga suman wa! Mikaketara oshiete kurê ya.*

Eh, I got into a hit-and-run. … The guy cuts into line at the gate, rams me, and then jets off! Shit! I gotta make him pay for repairs, at least. So tell me if you see the weasel!

V.T.: *Tokuchô wa?*

So how do I spot him?

Otto: *Soryâ <u>nô</u>, nantoka yû… Tôyô no megami san no e ga…*

Uh, lemme think. Yeah, there was this giant Asian goddess painted on his ship.

While V.T. and Otto are both blue-collar truckers, V.T. is a protagonist while Otto is a side character. V.T. is assigned SJ, while Otto is given Hiroshima dialect. The two different Japanese dialects function to project different characteristics — V.T. is normative and Otto is not. Most likely this harks back to the popular 1970s movie series *Torakku Yarô* 'Trucker Buddy' (Toei Video 2002–2009); the story was based in Hiroshima and the protagonist, Bunta Sugawara, acted in fluent Hiroshima dialect despite being from the Tôhoku region (see Figure 3).

Subsequently, both Sugawara and long-distance truckers became iconic images of Hiroshima dialect speakers especially in dramas and movies.

Hiroshima dialect belongs to a subgroup of western Japanese dialects distinct from SJ, which is itself a subdialect of eastern Japanese. Kinsui (2003) observed the language use of imaginary scientists/wise men from various films including Dr. Ochanomizu from *Astro Boy*, Dr. Agasa from *Meitantei Conan* 'Case Closed', Dr.

Figure 3. *Torakku Yarô*, Bunta Sugawara on the right

Ôkido from *Pokémon*, Professor Dumbledore of *Harry Potter*, and Master Yoda from *Star Wars* (in Japanese translations), and suggests that they are assigned a role language which he classifies as *hakasego* 'doctor/scientist language.' Kinsui (2003) also notes that *hakasego* contains many generic western Japanese characteristics.

Table 4. Hakasego 'doctor/scientist language' and SJ (adapted from Kinsui 2003:5)

Grammar	*Hakasego* 'doctor/scientist language'	SJ
Copula	*-ja and its variants*	*-da and its variants*
Negation marker	*-n/-nu*	*-nai*
Existential marker	*oru*	*iru*
Gerundive	*-tteoru/toru*	*-tteiru/iru*

Table 5. Generic characteristics of western and eastern Japanese (adapted from Kinsui 2003:5)

Grammar	Western Japanese	Eastern Japanese
Copula	*-ja/-ya and their variants*	*-da and its variants*
Negation marker	*-n/-hen*	*-nai/-nê*
Existential marker	*oru*	*iru*
Gerundive	*-tteoru/toru*	*-tteiru/iru*

CB as well contains its share of *hakasego*-speaking characters; in the following example, the chess master Hex, a brilliant, yet senile, scientist, converses with three other old men. In Example 7, Hex is talking about his new exciting chess mate.

(7) Hex and three old men, Episode 14: *Bohemian Rhapsody*
    Carlos: *Omaesan o tekozuraseru kurai ja yoppodo no yatsu jana!*
               He must be some player to pin you down!
    Hex: *Soreyori hirumeshi wa mada ka no?*
               I don't know. Let's have lunch first!
    Antonio: *Nani yûtoru? Sakki kûta jarôga!*
               You ate lunch a few minutes ago, blast it!
    Hex: *Hôjatta ka no?*
               Really? Did I like it?
    Jobin: *Boketorun janai ka?*
               You leave your brain somewhere? ·

Notice that it is not only Hex, but also the other old men who speak *hakasego*. Kinsui (2003:9) notes that old men speak just like doctors/scientists in manga or anime, and categorizes their speech as *rôjingo* 'old men's language'; he further notes that *hakasego* 'doctor/scientist language' is a subset of *rôjingo*, as only aged characters are assigned *hakasego*. Of note is the fact that young scientist characters in *CB* did not use *hakasego*. However, we occasionally meet knowledgeable old men who do not speak either *rôjingo* 'old men's language' or *hakasego* 'doctor/scientist language' — namely elderly villains in the series. Wang Long, Ping Long, and Sou Long are 120-year-old triplets and bosses of the Red Dragon triad. In Example 8, the elders are judging Vicious, the series' young main villain, who has betrayed the triad. They all speak SJ with formulaic expressions, highlighted with underlining in Example 8, which are not usually used in colloquial speech. Their speech sounds quite formal.

(8) The villains, Episode 25: *The Real Folk Blues 1*
     Wang Long: *Tonda dôke o yarakashita mono da. <u>Uranaishi ga kôitta. Akai</u>*
                  <u>tsuki no ban, hebi ga sono dokuga o furuô to osoroshiku hayaku</u>
                  <u>hashiru to</u>.
                  What a foolish thing this is that you have done. <u>A fortune-teller</u>
                  <u>warned us: On the night of the red moon, the snake will slither</u>
                  <u>and strike, bearing its venomous fangs.</u>
     Ping Long: *<u>Aware</u> ni mieru zo, Bishasu.*
                  You look so <u>pitiful</u>, Vicious. And you are.
     Sou Long: *Omae wa kôkeishaniwa narenai to <u>wareware</u> no kettei wa*
                  tsutaeta hazu da.
                  <u>We</u> have already informed you of our final decision. You cannot
                  succeed us as a leader of this clan.
     Vicious: *Tatakaukotono dekinai <u>shikabane</u> nado, soshikini wa hitsuyô nai.*
                  The syndicate doesn't need <u>corpses</u> that can't fight, who've lost
                  their taste for blood.

In *CB*, most of the villains speak in formal SJ as seen in Example 8. The triad elders, as iconic villains, align with normative villains rather than old men characters, despite the fact that they are 120 years old. In other words, their age is overshadowed by the iconization of their 'bad guy' traits. The formulaic speech used by the villains here is not idiosyncratic to *CB*; this kind of speech is often assigned to villains in other anime series. For example, in the first season of *Sailor Moon*, while most of the main female characters used JWL (including Sailor Moon and the Sailor Scouts), the ultimate enemy of Sailor Moon and the Scouts, Queen Beryl of the Negaverse, used this formal speech style more than any other character. Kristeva (1980:69) refers to texts in terms of two axes — a horizontal axis connects the author and reader of a text whereas a vertical axis links the text to other texts across time and space. In the same way that Otto the truck driver's language is intertextually linked to that of *Trucker Buddy*'s, the formal formulaic speech of the villains in *CB* is linked to other prior meanings. Satake (2003) states that while some types of role language are associated with prejudice and discrimination, another negative byproduct of role language is the reinforcement of normative language use or linguistic ideology, e.g. "what the correct Japanese language is" or "how should women and men speak" (Satake 2003:55).

5.   Foreigners' voices

We saw above that the *hakasego* or *rôjingo* characterization was withheld from certain otherwise eligible characters in favor of highlighting a different set of traits, namely their status as villains. This technique was further employed throughout the series, with the selection of aspects of various characters' personalities based on their ease of iconizability. One of the characters in the series, Laughing Bull, an aged Native American medicine man who consults Spike and Jet, also speaks very formulaic SJ, despite fitting both the age and wisdom criteria for *rôjingo/hakasego*.

> (9)   Laughing Bull to Jet, Episode 26: *The Real Folk Blues 2*
> Bull: *Hashiru iwa yo. Yatsu no hoshi wa nagareyôto shiteiru. Shi o osoreru na. Shi wa itsumo sobani iru. Osore o miseta totan, sore wa hikariyorimo hayaku tobikakatte kurudarô. Osorenakereba, sore wa tada yasashiku mimamotteiru dake da.*
> You, Running Rock. His star is about to fall. I have dreamed it. Do not fear death. Death is always at our side. When we show fear, it jumps at us faster than light. But if we do not show fear, it casts its eye upon us gently and then guides us into infinity.

The differences between the villains' language and Laughing Bull's is in the latter's rather long and complicated poetic expressions. Laughing Bull's lines are so abstract and metaphorical that they sound almost like the reciting of maxims rather than conversation. Meek (2006) discusses imaginary Native American characters' speech in the US and points out such clichés as the greeting 'how' accompanied by a raised hand, Indian calls or battle cries, and formulaic speech. In Japanese, stereotypical Native Americans often say things like *indian uso tsukanai* 'Indian no lie' or overuse formulaic names and metaphorical expressions, telltale signs of the influence of Hollywood movie translations. These expressions are equivalent to Kinsui's role language applied to Native Americans. In the case of Laughing Bull, his foreignness (as a Native American Indian) is more highlighted than his age or wisdom; therefore, the assignment of the stereotypical Native American expressions works to erase his other characteristics.

Other examples of role language assigned to obviously foreign characters include the speech of Chinese and Caucasian characters. Kinsui's descriptions of Chinese role language (2003:176–181; 2007:203–207) include omissions of case markers, as seen in the underlined sections of the following examples. The underlined parts are missing case markers; in line 1, *ninjin heisui (wa/de) genki (ga) jûbun yo* 'lit. ginseng tonic contains enough energy,' and line 2, *Isshûkan (wa) motsu* 'lit. it will last you a week.' These sentences would sound more native-Japanese when completed with the appropriate case markers.

(10)   Bartender and Hakim, Episode 2: *Stray Dog Strut*
      Bartender: *Nî-rai-rai. Okyaku-san, <u>ninjin **heisui** genki</u> jûbun yo.*
                        *<u>Isshûkan</u> motsu yo! Tsukareten nara satôkibi **heisui** yo!*
                        *Tabesugi dattara, painappuru **heisui** yo!*
                        Ni lai lai, if you feel rundown try some ginseng heisui. It'll keep you up for a week. Out of whack, try some sugar cane heisui. Ate too much? Have some pineapple heisui.
      Abdul Hakim: *Raochû da.*
                        Gimme some lao-chu.
      Bartender: *Shei shei. Hai yo!*
                        Thank you. Here you go.

Other than the case marker omissions, the overused sentence final particle *yo* as well as terms adopted from Chinese language (marked in boldface) aid in the indexing of the bartender in this example as a stereotypical Chinese character. The examples *nî-rai-rai* 'Mandarin, *ni lai lai*, lit. you come come,' *shei shei* 'Mandarin *xie xie*, lit. thank you,' and *heisui* 'Cantonese, soda/tonic, lit. gas water' are all quite obviously non-Japanese.

Japanese media also reserve a particular register of role language for Caucasian characters. The guest protagonist in one of the episodes, Andy von de Oniyate, is the heir to the wealthy Oniyate Ranch, but he chooses to be a bounty hunter because he believes it fits his cowboy-like cool nature. He has blond hair, blue eyes, and a penchant for cowboy fashion, appearing (if only superficially) as a typical Caucasian protagonist in a western movie. In her discussion of Caucasians' role language, Yoda (2007: 175–176) notes that use of interjections like *oh* or *ah*, as well as mixed English-Japanese expressions are stereotypical features of *seiyôjingo* 'westerners' language.' In Example 11, English words are inserted extensively into Andy's speech.

(11)   Andy, Episode 22: *Cowboy Funk*
      [at a crime scene, suspecting Spike to be a culprit]
      ANDY: *Kyô kokoni bakudan o shikakeruto yuukoto wa, <u>you</u> no hanzai shûki o keisansureba, <u>me</u> niwa kantan ni wakarukoto da.*
               I figured that you'd plant an explosive here today. It wasn't difficult after I studied your crime patterns and profiled your criminal mind.
      [at a crime scene, being unsuspicious of a real culprit]
      ANDY: *Kare wa <u>gâdoman</u> janai ka!*

> Yeah right, that old security guard.
>
> [justifying an entrance of his horse to a party]
>
> ANDY: *Oh, my aiba, Onikisu wa, tada no uma dewa nai!*
>
> Oh ho! But my Onyx is no ordinary steed!
>
> [at a party, boasting his cowboy qualities to Faye]
>
> ANDY: *Sô! Watashi wa sonna koto ki ni shinai! Kore to kimetara, hoka wa nothing, mienai no sa.*
>
> Ma'am, I can't worry about that. When my mind is set, well I'm wearin' blinders. Nothing else matters!
>
> [at a crime scene, questioning a culprit]
>
> ANDY: *Omae wa dare da? Who are you?!*
>
> What do you want? Who are you?!

The expression seen in the 2nd excerpt, *kare* 'he,' while a Japanese word, sounds like a direct translation from English and adds qualitative non-nativeness. In Example 12, another Caucasian character, Judy, again exemplifies *seiyôjingo* features such as English vocabulary mixing and the unnatural use of pronouns.

(12) Judy, Episode 12: *Jupiter Jazz 1*

Judy: *Ûn! Good news wa, shôkin ga odoroki no, happakumantte koto ne! ... Karetteba tôttemo suteki nanoyo!*

Mmm, and the good news is he's worth a whopping eight million woolongs! ...What a handsome guy!

Both Andy and Judy's *seiyôjingo*, which is highlighted in Examples 11 and 12, helps to construct a sense of foreignness, which is not the same as the foreignness projected by the Native American or Chinese characters presented above as each of them indexes different types of foreignerness — the Native American, Chinese, and Caucasian.

6. Conclusions: Hegemonic normativity, iconization, and naturalization

Based on the observations of the Japanese language in *CB*, I argue that both normative and non-normative characters are constructed to conform with hegemonic ideals of gender, sexuality, occupation, age, and race. Normative characters are represented as possessing most or all ideal traits, both visually and linguistically, as the artwork and speech of both heroes and babes reflect. At the same time, characters that do not conform to desirable sexual, visual, national, or age norms are rendered less than attractive and are assigned linguistic features that deviate from colloquial SJ. Of the four main characters, Spike, Jet, and Faye have speech styles which serve to perpetuate the generic ideals of hegemonic normativity. The good guys' tough language (tougher even than their enemies) and near-invincibility successfully iconize the heroes' expected attributes while the babes, although occasionally lapsing into unladylike expressions and behaviors, otherwise maintain a speech style indexing their femininity. Additionally, normative guest protagonists demonstrate their heroic attributes and, despite their tendency to die at the end, prove nearly invincible until the very end of the show. All episodes are based on dominant ideology and are predictable, appealing to a wide range of audiences both Japanese and non-Japanese. As mentioned earlier, the widespread acceptance of a dominant ideology owes its success to its ability to convince people that it is not a matter of ideology, but simply natural, the way things are (Eckert and McConnell-Ginet 2003:43). This process of naturalization presents normativity as something that needs no explanation. Naturalized ideas like 'it is just natural for men to be macho and women to be babes,' are rampant in pop culture. Of course, anime is patently fiction with overly exaggerated characters and it is not a direct reflection of the way things are in reality. Anime, like many other pop culture consumables such as comics and cartoons, seems to belong to a genre that lends itself to irony and reflexivity. Nonetheless, as discussed by Satake (2003), writing on gendered language use in children's anime programs, anime as a genre does influence reinforcement of hegemonic norms, leading to prejudice, discrimination, and linguistic prescriptivism. For example, an oversimplified iconization process drew international attention to a particular anime program in 2008. The popular anime show *Jojo no Kimyô na Bôken* '*Jojo's Bizarre Adventure*' (Studio A.P.P.P. 1993/2001, Original by Hirohiko Araki), was criticized for including an anti-Muslim innuendo when one of the story's villains, while reading the Koran in front of a mosque-like structure, orders his subordinates to murder the protagonists; international Muslim communities attacked the show for propagating a crude equation between the Koran and the 'bad guys' (Japan Times 2008). Yet this kind of iconization does get disseminated easily across cultures via popular media such as anime. At the same time, the global acceptance of the hegemonically naturalized norms may contribute to the success of anime, a medium which tends to convey rather stereotypical and simplistic stories in naturalized terms.

In her summary of gendered speech styles, Cameron (1997:49) mentions that "[w]hereas sociolinguistics traditionally assumes that people talk the way they do because of who they (already) are, the postmodernist approach suggests that people are who they are because of (among other things) the way they talk." Pennycook (2003:528) mirrors this line of thought, referring to performativity and pre-existing identities, and states that "[i]t is not that people use language varieties because of who they are, but rather that we perform who we are by (amongst other things) using varieties of language." The *CB* characters, as with all scripted characters, are created with preconceived identities and appearances, and this determines their language use. As all of the characters share futuristic bohemian backgrounds, their individual particulars, such as ethnicity and language, are kept vague throughout the show. It is the language that projects their fictional identities. The default viewers being Japanese at the time of production, the protagonists do not fail to speak SJ and have culture-specific knowledge of Japan regardless of their apparently non-Japanese names and appearances; however, detailed ethnicities or language backgrounds are not mentioned. The mainstream characters are just assumed to be aligned to a default 'normative Japanese' category. There are more than a few episodes in which the main characters behave as if they were Japanese natives by demonstrating their understanding of traditional information such as traditional stories, cuisine, maxims, cultural values, etc. Additionally, even though as the series progresses, it is revealed that Faye Valentine is actually Singaporean, her native Japanese fluency does not betray any such foreignness, unlike the case of other supposedly non-Japanese characters such as the Chinese bartender, the Native American medicine man, or the American cowboy. Her 'pre-existing identity' as the show's central female character dictates that she will have the iconic language which is expected for her role. The SJ, as well as the JWL, that she manipulates natively, indexes her mainstream position throughout the series. The same can be said of any incongruities regarding other characters in the show. The obvious foreigners are saddled with non-SJ or non-native Japanese fluency which iconize their foreign roles. In short, pre-existing identities are paired with the appropriate role language to reinforce the stratification of linguistic registers.

Blommaert (2003:611) writes that there is a "worldwide lingua-cultural homogenization" taking place, with western norms becoming global norms, manifested in such ways as the modern Japanese language's frequent use of English as well as adaptations of western cultures. Referring to this phenomenon as '*McDonaldization*,' Blommaert (2003:611) states that it "allows language users opportunities to represent cultural, social, and historical conditions of being." The rapid penetration of anime into the global market, in contrast, may well be observed as the Japanese counterpart to this McDonaldization: a Japanese pop culture commodity absorbed into a transnational culture and being appropriated as a part of a hegemonic norm.

Acknowledgements

I gratefully acknowledge the financial and institutional support given to this project by the National University of Singapore FASS Start-up Grant (AY2008-1). Parts of this paper were presented at the 108th American Anthropological Association's Annual Meeting in Philadelphia in December 2009, in the panel 'Media intertextualities: semiotic mediation across time and space,' which was co-organized by Joseph Park and me. I thank the audience for their feedback. My sincere thanks also go to Jacob Mey, Hartmut Haberland, and Kerstin Fischer as well as two reviewers for their helpful suggestions and comments on earlier versions of this article. I am also appreciative of Yukiko Ogawa and Yuichi Endo of SUNRISE Inc. International Branch and Ikko Kawamura of Toei Co. International Division and Toei Co., who kindly supplied me with the artwork used in this paper. I am especially indebted to Asif Agha, Laurie Durand, Benjamin George, Joseph Park, and Lionel Wee for their invaluable assistance and encouragement at various stages of this project.

DVD

Cowboy Bebop: Complete Session Collection. 2003. [video] Directed by Shinichiro Watanabe. USA: Pioneer Video. [6 videodiscs (10hr., 50 min.)]

References

Abe, Hideko. 2004. Lesbian Bar Talk in Shinjuku, Tokyo. In: Japanese Language, Gender, and Identity, Shigeko Okamoto and Janet Shibamoto Smith (eds), 205–221. New York: Oxford University Press.

Agha, Asif. 2005. Voice, Footing, Enregisterment. Journal of Linguistic Anthropology 15, 1, 38–59.

Allison, Anne. 2000. Sailor Moon: Japanese superheroes for global girls. In: Japan Pop!: Inside the world of Japanese popular culture, Timothy J. Craig (ed), 259–278. Armonk, New York: M.E. Sharpe.

Anderson, Benedict. 1983. Imagined Communities: Reflections on the origin and spread of nationalism. London: Verso.

Blommaert, Jan. 2003. Commentary: A sociolinguistics of globalization. Journal of Sociolinguistics 7, 607–623.

Cameron, Deborah. 1997. Performing Gender Identity: Young men's talk and the construction of heterosexual masculinity. In: Language and Masculinity, Sally Jonson and Ulrike H. Meinhof (eds), 47–64. Oxford: Blackwell.

Cameron, Deborah and Don Kulick. 2003. Language and Sexuality. Cambridge: Cambridge University Press.

Cornog, Martha and Timothy Perper. 2005. Non-western Sexuality Comes to the U.S.: A crash course in manga and anime for sexologists. Contemporary Sexuality 39, 3, 1–6.

Eckert, Penelope. 2002. Demystifying Sexuality and Desire. In: Language and Sexuality: Contesting meaning in theory and practice, Kathryn Campbell-Kibler, Robert Podesva, Sarah Roberts, and Andrew Wong (eds), 99–110. Stanford, California: CSLI.

Eckert, Penelope and Sally McConnell-Ginet. 2003. Language and Gender. Cambridge: Cambridge University Press.

Foucault, Michel. 1980. Power/Knowledge: Selected interviews and other writings. New York: Pantheon.

Fushimi, Noriaki. 1991. Puraibêto Gei Raifu: Posto ren'airon [A Private Gay Life: Post-love theory]. Tokyo: Gakuyô Shobô.

Gal, Susan. 1995. Language, Gender, and Power: An anthropological review. In: Gender Articulated: Language and the socially constructed self, Kira Hall and Mary Bucholtz (eds), 169–82. New York: Routledge.

Gal, Susan. 1998. Multiplicity and Contention among Language Ideologies: A commentary. In Language Ideologies: Practice and theory, Bambi Schieffelin, Kathryn Woolard and Paul Kroskrity (eds), 317–331. Oxford: Oxford University Press.

Gal, Susan and Judith Irvine. 1995. The Boundaries of Languages and Disciplines: How ideologies construct difference. Social Research 62, 967–1001.

Gaubatz, Thomas M. 2007. Translating Dialect in Mark Twain's The Adventures of Huckleberry Finn. In: Yakuwarigo Kenkyû no Chihei [Horizons of Role-language Research], Satoshi Kinsui (ed), 125–158. Tokyo: Kuroshio.

Hall, Kira. 1995. Lip Service on the Fantasy Lines. In: Gender Articulated: Language and the socially constructed self, Kira Hall and Mary Bucholtz (eds), 183–216. New York: Routledge.

Hill, Jane. 2005. Intertextuality as Source and Evidence for Indirect Indexical Meanings. Journal of Linguistic Anthropology 15, 1, 113–124.

Hiramoto, Mie. 2009. Slaves Speak Pseudo-Tôhoku-ben: The representation of minorities in the Japanese translation of Gone with the Wind. Journal of Sociolinguistics 13, 2, 249–263.

Ide, Sachiko. 1982. Japanese Sociolinguistics: Politeness and women's language. Lingua 57, 357–385.

Inoue, Miyako. 2003. Speech Without a Speaking Body: 'Japanese women's language' in translation. Language & Communication 23, 315–330.

Japan Times. 2008. 'Anime' Stokes Ire of Muslims: Shueisha freezes sales as critics slam 'JoJo's Bizarre' Quran scene Cairo, May 23, News section, Online edition. http://search.japantimes. co.jp/cgi-bin/nn20080523a1.html

Kiesling, Scott F. 2002/2006. Playing the Straight Man: Displaying and maintaining male heterosexuality in discourse. In: The Language and Sexuality Reader, Deborah Cameron and Don Kulick (eds), 118–131. London and New York: Routledge.

Kiesling, Scott F. 2005. Homosocial Desire in Men's Talk: Balancing and re-creating cultural discourses of masculinity. Language in Society, 34, 695–726.

Kinsui, Satoshi. 2003. Bâcharu Nihongo: Yakuwarigo no nazo [Virtual Japanese: The mystery of role-language]. Tokyo: Iwanami.

Kinsui, Satoshi (ed). 2007. Yakuwarigo Kenkyû no Chihei [Horizons of Role-language Research]. Tokyo: Kuroshio.

Kristeva, Julia. 1980. Desire in Language: A semiotic approach to literature and art. New York: Columbia University Press.

Lippi-Green, Rosina. 1997. English with an Accent: Language, ideology, and discrimination in the United States. London and New York: Routledge.

Maio, Kathi. 2003. Films. Fantasy & Science Fiction. September, 94–98.

McGloin, Naomi. 1990. Sex Difference and Sentence-final Particles. In: Aspects of Japanese Women's Language, Sachiko Ide and Naomi McGloin (eds), 23–41. Tokyo: Kuroshio.

Meek, Barbra. 2006. And the Injun Goes 'How!': Representations of American Indian English in white public space. Language in Society 35, 93–128.

Napier, Susan. 2005. Anime from Akira to Howl's Moving Castle: Experiencing contemporary Japanese animation. New York: Palgrave.

Ochs, Elinor. 1992. Indexing Gender. In: Rethinking Context: Language as an interactive phenomenon, Alessandro Duranti and Charles Goodwin (eds), 335–358. Cambridge: Cambridge University Press.

Okamoto, Shigeko. 1995. 'Tasteless' Japanese: Less 'feminine' speech among young Japanese women. In: Gender Articulated: Language and the socially constructed self, Kira Hall and Mary Bucholtz (eds), 297–325. New York: Routledge.

Park, Joseph Sung-Yul. 2009. Regimenting Languages on Korean Television: Subtitles and institutional authority. Text & Talk 29, 5, 547–570.

Pennycook, Alastair. 2003. Global Englishes, Rip Slyme, and Performativity. Journal of Sociolinguistics 7, 513–533.

Reynolds, Katsue. 1985. Female Speakers of Japanese. Feminist Issues 5, 13–46.

Satake, Kuniko. 2003. Terebi Anime no Rufusuru 'Onna Kotoba/Otoko Kotoba' Kihan [Women's Language/Men's Language Guidelines Spread through Television Anime Shows]. Kotoba [Language] 24, 43–59.

Shibamoto, Janet. 1985. Japanese Women's Language. Orlando, Florida: Academic Press.

Studio A.P.P.P. 1993/2001. Jojo no Kimyô na Bôken 3 [Jojo's Bizarre Adventure 3]. [video] Directed by Hiroyuki Kitakubo and Hideki Futamura, Original by Hirohiko Araki. Tokyo: Kadokawa Entertainment. [5 videodiscs (7hr., 30 min.)]

Suzuki, Chizu. 1998. 'Joseigo' o Tayôsuru Dansei wa 'Okama' ka? [Are Men who Frequently Use Women's Language 'Queers'?] Kotoba [Language] 19, 69–91.

Toei Animation. 1992/2002. Bishôjosenshi Sailor Moon 1 [Pretty Soldier Sailor Moon 1]. [video] Directed by Jun'ichi Satô, Original by Naoko Takeuchi. Tokyo: Toei. [1 videodisc (1hr., 25 min.)]

Toei Video. 2002–2009. Torakku Yarô Sirîzu [Trucker Buddy Series]. [video] Directed by Noribumi Suzuki. Tokyo: Toei. [10 videodiscs total (approximately 1 hr., 20 min. each)]

Wee, Lionel. 2006. The Semiotics of Language Ideologies in Singapore. Journal of Sociolinguistics 10, 344–361.

Yoda, Megumi. 2007. Seiyôjingo "Ô, Romio!" no Bunkei: Sono kakuritsu to fukyû [The Sentence Pattern "Oh, Romeo!" as Westerner Language: Its establishment and spread]. In: Yakuwari-go Kenkyû no Chihei [Horizons of Role-language Research], Satoshi Kinsui (ed), 159–178. Tokyo: Kuroshio.

Yoshimeki, Haruhiko. 1993. Sekiryô Kôya [Solitude Point]. Bungei Shunjû [Literature Art Spring-Autumn]. September, 410–469.

Intertextuality, mediation, and members' categories in focus groups on humor

Toshiaki Furukawa
Osaka University

This paper extends studies on intertextuality into a more explicitly interactional context. I examine the actual process of intertextuality where comedy audiences construct recombinant selves through making sense of various membership categories as well as through making sense of a certain kind of comedy. The examination of this process requires receptive research; however, most studies leave the interpretive process unanalyzed. Conducting both a sequential analysis and a membership categorization analysis will reveal that categories are not "pre-formed" but "per-formed" in situ. To illustrate these points, I report on a receptive study of Local comedy in Hawai'i.

1. Introduction

Mediation is an intertextual and dialogic process in which various categories are generated and are interpreted by interactants. The mediating process enables interactants to align with, or to disalign from, one another as well as other members of a society in the formation of community; this process also arguably reinforces linguistic and ethnic stereotyping. The examination of mediation requires receptive research, which often uses focus groups as a data generating method; however, most studies conduct content analysis, leaving the interactional, interpretive process unanalyzed. Taking a sequential analysis approach to focus group data (Edwards and Stokoe 2004; Wilkinson 2004, 2008) will reveal that categories are not "pre-formed" but "per-formed" in situ (Puchta and Potter 2004). To illustrate these points, I examine the interpretive process of membership categories (Sacks 1979) among Local comedy audiences in Hawai'i.[1] As Blake (1996) conceptualizes humor in Hawai'i as interethnic humor, I chose Hawai'i comedy because this

---

1. I make a distinction between a 'little l' local and a 'big L' Local throughout this paper to isolate Local residents from long-term local residents who are not from Hawai'i. A stereotypical Local is a descendant of plantation laborers and must be born and raised in Hawai'i.

culturally-specific genre constitutes a multilingual, multicultural, and multiracial niche of identity management within broader political-economic dimensions of media circulation; thus, this study also contributes to the discussion of crosscultural membership categorization in mass mediation.

The present article is not about the media product per se, but about how media products such as comedians and comedy clips can effectively be "stance objects" (Du Bois 2007) towards which focus group participants orient and construct personal and collective identities. The object of stance is "what the evaluation is about" (Du Bois 2007: 149); and it can be knowledge, emotion, membership categories, or category-bound actions/attributes. The paper investigates people's metaperformance talk and extends studies on intertextuality into a more explicitly interactional context, in line with recent work that explores semiotic chains that contribute to figures of personhood (e.g., Agha 2007a, b, this issue).

2.   Literature review

Focus group interviews have been widely used for various purposes (Krueger and Casey 2009; Morgan 2002), from market research (Puchta and Potter 2004) and public opinion polling (Myers 2007) to social science studies. The goal of a focus group is "to collect data that is of interest to the researcher — typically to find the range of opinions of people across several groups" (Krueger and Casey 2009: 7). However, in focus group research, content analysis has been dominant while interactional meaning has long been neglected (e.g., Peek and Fothergill 2009; Pösö et al. 2008).

The focus group interview is a site for the production of meaning, not simply a site for the collection of data. It is an occasion for participants "to *construct* versions of reality interactionally rather than merely purvey data" (Gubrium and Holstein 2002: 14, emphasis in original). The discursive analyst's goal is not to reveal the truthfulness of what the participants say, but to examine the construction of "believability" (Potter 1996). Moreover, the interview is reflexive in the sense that it develops "as each participant looks at the world through the other's eyes, incorporating both self and other into the process of interpretation" (Warren 2002: 98). I investigate the construction of such versions of reality through my research of interviews as talk-in-interaction. Furthermore, I do not isolate *what* is constructed from *how* it is constructed, as both are components of meaning-making (Baker 2003; Edwards 1991; Gubrium & Holstein 2002; Roulston 2006).

Potter and Hepburn (2005) identify two sets of problems with qualitative interviewing from a conversation analytically (CA)-influenced perspective of discursive psychology: the first deals with contingent problems in the design, conduct, and presentation of interviews; and the second has to do with necessary, or unavoidable, problems in the analysis of interviews. These problems are summarized in Table 1.

Table 1. Problems in the design, conduct, presentation, and analysis of qualitative interviews (Potter and Hepburn 2005:19)

Contingent problems	Necessary problems
(1) the deletion of the interviewer	(1) the flooding of the interview with social
(2) the conventions of representation of interaction	science agendas and categories
	(2) the complex and varying footing positions
(3) the specificity of observations	of interviewer and interviewee
(4) the unavailability of the interview set-up	(3) the possible stake and interest of interviewer and interviewee
(5) the failure to consider interviews as interaction	(4) the reproduction of cognitivism

Using a CA-informed transcription and analytic conventions, I attempt to resolve all of these five contingent problems. On the other hand, none of the four necessary problems can be dealt with entirely satisfactorily (Potter and Hepburn 2005). I attend closely to participants' orientations in order to minimize these latter, necessary analytic problems.

Agha (2007a) discusses context-bound categorization with respect to time and space, and he refers to discursive products of this chronotopic action as "recombinant selves." Recombinant selves are not concrete individuals but more abstract "social-characterological types" (Agha 2007a:333); such types are performed figures of subjectivity, are dialogically configured, and are delineated through contrasts. Agha (2007a) also suggests that social types may have mass appeal for individual consumers. Recombinant selves are generated through a semiotic encounter in which signs such as utterances, gestures, and text-artifacts connect people to one another; moreover, "[s]emiotic encounters are *mass mediated* when the signs that connect persons to each other connect *many* persons to each other within unified participation frameworks (through a common orientation to those signs)" (Agha 2007a:325, emphasis in original).

Both focus group interviews and comedy shows — as discussed by the focus group participants — constitute a site of mass mediation where, I argue, the participants share a common orientation to cultural signs and become connected to one another — and even to other members that they may not know. Since the focus group participants talk about their interpretation of Local humor, this activity inevitably involves "cross-linkages of language in use" (Spitulnik 2001:95) or intertextuality (i.e., every text such as a statement and an utterance displays links with previous as well as synchronic texts; Blommaert 2005). In her discussion of the social circulation of media discourse in popular culture, Spitulnik states rightly that "we learn little about the practices of consumption and even less about what people are saying to each other about their experiences of consumption" (Spitulnik 2001: 97), and claims that the recycling of media discourse serves as a crucial component in the formation of community. I reconceptualize the construction of a recombinant self (Agha 2007a) as a situated — or decontextualized and recontextualized (Bauman and Briggs 1990) — interactional categorization through which interactants manage their "social relations" (Agha 2007b).

Hence, I take a membership categorization analysis approach (Sacks 1979) as my chief analytical tool and examine the emergence of membership categories in focus group interviews as talk-in-interaction. Membership categories (e.g., man, woman, husband, wife, etc.) are neither exclusive nor neutral descriptions; they are "culturally available resources which allow us to describe, identify or make reference to other people or to ourselves" (Hutchby and Wooffitt 2008: 35). In addition, based on Zimmerman (1998), I distinguish three kinds of identity: portable (e.g., 'Asian'), situational (e.g., 'moderator'), and discursive (e.g., 'white-washed Asian').

3. Methods

I designed a focus group study following the guidelines in Krueger and Casey (2009), and conducted four focus group interviews in November, 2008, at the University of Hawai'i at Mānoa campus. These one-shot focus group interviews were semi-structured and lasted for one hour. I set two requirements for participants: they had to (1) be born and raised in Hawai'i, and (2) have been to Local comedy shows or have watched Local comedy TV programs, videos, DVDs, etc.[2] Nineteen participants (13 females and 6 males in their 20s–50s) were recruited on a friend-of-a-friend basis, as well as through advertising on the university campus. Each

---

2. Local comedy has been recognized as a genre since the 1950s and 1960s. One of the landmarks in the history of Local comedy was when Rap Reiplinger won an Emmy Award in 1982 for a TV special *Rap's Hawai'i* that was released as a video and, later, as a DVD. Reiplinger has been given a legendary status since his untimely death in 1984; for instance, some of the clips from his show were uploaded to YouTube, and as of July in 2010, the most popular clip, *Aunty Marialani's Cooking Show*, has been watched over 93,000 times in less than three years. Other comedians who became popular in the late 1970s and 1980s include Frank DeLima, Andy Bumatai, and Mel Cabang. They still perform at comedy shows, host TV programs, or appear in TV commercials, bringing back good memories to many people. Shawn Kaui Hill is another well-known comedian who performed the Hawai'i Creole speaking character Bu Lai'a. His fame or infamy reached its peak when he ran for governor of Hawai'i in the 1990s and received 5,761 votes in the Democratic gubernatorial primary (Yuen, 1998). Popular among younger audiences are Da Braddahs — whose TV show *Da Braddahs & Friends* is aired on OC16 — and Augie T (See Appendix). The popularity of the above comedians is partly attested by the fact that their CDs and DVDs are readily available in retail stores.

group consisted of four to six participants plus a research assistant and myself. The research assistant, who also met the above criteria, took notes during each session in order to provide a brief, two-to-three-minute-long summary of the discussion to the group at the end of the session. All the groups contained a pre-existing group of friends, but no group consisted only of such a group. In addition, three out of the four focus groups included at least one participant who already knew the researcher (as a friend, a student, etc.) prior to the focus group session. Each session was audio recorded with a Sony IC Recorder ICD-SX46. The four hours of recordings were transcribed for further analysis according to the Jeffersonian CA conventions.

Each session started with my self-introduction and explanation of the research. This was followed by my confirmation of the requirements. I emphasized that the participants were the "specialists" on Local comedy. (I served as the moderator and introduced myself as an international graduate student from Japan.) When this was done, the participants were asked to introduce themselves by telling the group their names and the last time they had gone to a Local comedy show. When the introductions ended, I announced that they were free to comment in any order, and the participants were encouraged to respond to each other. I then asked the following open questions: (1) What is the first thing that comes to mind when you hear the phrase "Local comedy"?; and (2) Who is your favorite Local comedian? Each question was discussed for a few minutes. Following this, a DVD clip and three audio clips were played.

The first clip is a pseudo-skit titled *Room Service* in Rap Reiplinger's DVD *Rap's Hawai'i*. Reiplinger plays two roles in this clip: a Local telephone operator at a hotel, possibly, in Waikiki and a white tourist who asks for room service; however, this interaction generates a great deal of miscommunication. The second clip is a parody song by Frank DeLima, *Christmas Carol (Filipino Christmas)*. It is a medley of Christmas songs in which many linguistic and cultural stereotypes about Filipinos are incorporated. The third clip is a track, *Non Ethnic Joke*, from Andy Bumatai's CD that was recorded at his live stand-up comedy show in Waikiki. In this clip, Bumatai describes three characters at a bar each of whom shows stereotypical behaviors of their ethnicity, but Bumatai does not refer to the ethnic categories — Filipino, Portuguese, and Chinese — that his jokes are about. The fourth and last clip is taken from Augie T's live stand-up comedy show. In this clip, he talks about some people who are offended by his jokes, which leads to another joke. In order to give the reader some idea of Local stand-up comedy, I have included this clip as an appendix.

After each clip, I asked the group "What do you think about this clip?" Usually there would be discussion for several minutes, and then the next clip would be played. After all four clips had been played and briefly discussed, the participants were asked to respond to the following three open, more focused questions: (1) Who do you think would not be able to understand this kind of comedy? (2) Who do you think would dislike this kind of comedy? and (3) What would you say to somebody who may claim that this kind of comedy is not politically correct? Finally, I asked one more question: If you had to name one thing, what allows you to enjoy Local comedy the most? A brief spoken summary of the discussion was provided at the end by the research assistant to allow for feedback from the participants. After the session, each participant was asked to fill out a basic demographic survey.

My own three research questions are the following: (1) How do the focus group participants make sense of Local comedy? (2) What do the participants talk

Table 2. Focus group participants

Group	Excerpts	Name	Age	Sex	Ethnicity[4]
1	2	Andy	20s	M	Chinese
		H-Mom	40s	F	Hawaiian, Native American, Spanish [5]
		J	20s	M	Filipino
		Kaimana	20s	F	Filipino, Hawaiian, Portuguese
		Michi	20s	F	Chinese, Japanese, Korean, Okinawan
		T	40s	M	Hawaiian, Other[6]
2	n/a	Angel	20s	F	Filipino
		Chris	20s	M	Japanese, White
		Clara	20s	F	Filipino
		Jessica	20s	F	Filipino
		Katie	20s	F	Chinese, Hawaiian, Portuguese, White, Spanish, Native American[7]
3	3	Craig	30s	M	Chinese, Filipino, Hawaiian, White
		Kekoa	40s	M	Chinese, Hawaiian, White
		Kristy	20s	F	Japanese
		Sarah	40s	F	Chinese, Hawaiian, White
4	1	Akemi	30s	F	Chinese, Hawaiian, Japanese
		Jill	20s	F	Japanese, Okinawan
		Judee	50s	F	Japanese
		Mary	50s	F	Chinese, Filipino, Portuguese, White

3. The survey listed the following ethnic categories: Chinese, Filipino, Hawaiian, Japanese, Korean, Okinawan, Portuguese, White (i.e., European/Haole), and Other. Based on ethnographic knowledge, Portuguese was listed as an independent category from White. The former is often treated as such in Hawai'i because they served as *luna*s (foremen) in the plantation.

4. H-Mom added Native American and Spanish.

5. T provided no specific category for Other.

6. Katie added Spanish and Native American.

about as stance objects? and (3) How do the participants show sensitivity to inter-textual links with previous or relevant media discourses? It should be noted here that my objective is not to generalize about what Local people think about Local comedy; rather, I consider focus group participants as members of a community that understand a certain type of comedy in Hawai'i. They may not only under-stand, but even enjoy this type of comedy partly because I recruited them under the two conditions stated earlier. Nevertheless, I investigate how they construct their attitudes — positive, negative, or both — in focus groups as talk-in-interac-tion. My goal is to illuminate the actual process of intertextuality through analyz-ing the interaction in focus groups on humor and identifying how the focus group participants make connections between micro and macro contexts. A summary of the focus group participants' backgrounds is given in Table 2.[7]

4.   Interpretive frames

A repertoire of interpretive frames is a system of values and categories that mem-bers of a community use to achieve intersubjectivity about reality. In the pres-ent context, this system of meaning-making emerges in talk-in-interaction when the participants of the four focus groups discuss their interpretations of the media clips. The participants also introduce relevant categories and values and develop them further throughout the focus group sessions. The excerpts below show a culturally-specific interpretive repertoire that includes: doing being Local (Excerpt 1); white-washed (Excerpt 2); and a different kind of humor (Excerpt 3).

4.1 Doing being Local

Excerpt 1 (ll. 1–57) is taken from a group with four participants: Akemi, Jill, Judee, and Mary. After the discussion of the clip they had just listened to, I (TF) asked the participants, "Who do you think would not be able to understand this kind of com-edy?" The participants discussed this question, and when their discussion was over, I asked, "Who do you think would dislike this kind of comedy?" Instead of answer-ing this question, the participants went back to the previous question. The excerpt starts when Judee responds to TF's question by posing her own question to Mary.

Excerpt 1a "He is a Local boy"
1   Judee   you think <°blacks would understand it°>?
2   Mary   m:::: I- * <bla:cks>,

---

7. All names are pseudonyms.

```
3           I get- I don't (.) <have many black friends>
4           and [I just don't know
5  Judee       [yeah me too
6  Mary   what they find (.) [humorous?
7  Judee                    [funny. fu- funny or,
8           (.2)
9  Mary   although my (.) husband did °go to school
10          with Barack Obama:°.
11 TF     uh huh.
12 All     ((laughter))
```

Judee introduces a new membership category (i.e., "blacks") that has not been mentioned by anyone in the group (including myself). Her question about this category turns out to be a trouble source: Mary initiates her response with great difficulty in line 2. Rather than answering Judee's question right away, Mary states that she does not have many black friends. She disqualifies herself from providing an answer to Judee's question in line 4. Judee aligns with Mary in line 5 by revealing that she does not have many black friends, either. A short pause in line 8 is followed by Mary's utterance in line 9, where she provides an anecdote that even though she does not have many black friends, her husband is acquainted with someone who belongs to this category. TF produces a minimal response in line 11, and the laughter of all the participants except TF in line 12 treats Mary's utterance (that is closed with the introduction of the proper noun, i.e., Barack Obama) as accountable. Mary treats this proper noun as referring to someone who went to school with her husband and who is classified into a group of "blacks" or "black friends." Thus, she creates the possibility that her utterance about them (e.g., "and [I just don't know what they find (.) [humorous?") may not be 'true,' given what the participants would know about Barack Obama as a public figure who became a president-elect a few weeks before this focus group session.

In the next excerpt, Mary accounts for the introduction of "Barack Obama" in her telling.

Excerpt 1b

```
13     Mary    uhm (.4) but even him (.)
14     TF      uh huh.
15     Mary    being you know,
16             well he's like you know white and black,
17             but (.4) being raised here, (.8)
18             we have so much (.2) in common.
19             we can understand him and .h (1.0) I don't know,
```

---

8. Paka or pakalōlō is a term for marijuana used in Hawai'i.

20		[he's just (.) you know?
21	TF	[uh huh.
22		(.8)
23	Mary	not to bring this into a political (.4)
24		[kind of situation,
25	TF	[uh huh.
26	Mary	but you know, even he: (.) has the ties to Hawaiʻi
27		and (.) .h we just feel so connected to him.
28	TF	uh huh.
29	Mary	you know,
30		and he did all those things like
31		<going to the beach and (.)
32		↓smoking paka:>,[8]
33		and (.) £doing all these things you know£?
34		[<he is a Local boy>.
35	TF	[uh huh.

Mary restarts her telling about "him" (i.e., "Barack Obama") in line 13. She treats him as someone distant from her by saying "even him." She modifies her interpretation of the ethnicity of "Barack Obama" in line 16, re-categorizing him as "white and black." Mary briefly describes his life history (i.e., "being raised here") in a way that enables her to say that "we have so much in common." She refers to herself as "we," thereby identifying herself as a member of a group of people who are from "here" and "can understand him." Producing a series of hedgings towards the end of the line,[9] Mary accounts for what is "so much in common" (l. 18) by stating that even Barack Obama "has the ties to Hawaiʻi" in line 26 and that people in Hawaiʻi "just feel so connected to him." Mary specifies category-bound activities (i.e., "going to the beach" and "smoking paka") in lines 31 and 32, all of which she claims Barack Obama did in the past. She asserts in line 34 that he is "a Local boy," a category to which the preceding activities are connected. By making Barack Obama a Local, Mary achieves categorizing herself as a Local, too, because she mentions repeatedly that "we" have so much in common with him. The next sequence begins with a question that TF asks to the participants.

---

9. One of the reviewers pointed out that Mary's utterance in lines 23–24 (i.e., "not to bring this into a political (.4) kind of situation") orients to the politicized debates about Obama's racial identity during the presidential campaign, thus providing evidence that at least Mary sees the ongoing talk as linked with such prior media discourses. However, this could also be her orienting to a norm that political discussions should be inappropriate for a discussion on Local humor, which is how the focus group was framed.

Excerpt 1c

36	TF	do you think uh (.8) Barack Obama
37		would understand this kind of (.) kind of (.) comedy?
38	Mary	yeah.
39	Akemi	yes.
40	Judee	yeah he would.
41	Jill	I do.

Building upon Mary's categorization of Barack Obama as a Local boy, TF poses a closed question about his ability to understand Local comedy in lines 36 and 37. All the participants respond to this question one after another with affirmative answers in lines 38–41.

Excerpt 1d

42		(.4)
43	Mary	he was here long enough you know?
44		he, he, you know? (.6)
45		he did all these things. you know,
46		hanging out with his buddies,
47		and every[thing going surfing and doing whatevers,
48	TF	[uh huh.
49		(.6)
50	Mary	so:, yeah. (.4) he can relate?
51	TF	uh huh.
52	Mary	you know?

After a 0.4 second pause, Mary takes the floor in line 43 and starts to account for her response in the previous excerpt. She states that Barack Obama lived in Hawai'i long enough (to become a Local boy), and that he performed the category-bound activities that characterize being a Local. After a 0.6 second pause in line 49, Mary restarts a closing sequence in line 50 (i.e., "so:,") and concludes that "he can relate" with a rising intonation, finishing her assertion of why Obama should be able to appreciate the jokes. In the next excerpt, TF asks a confirmation question about Mary's interpretation.

Excerpt 1e

53	TF	does everybody agree?
54	Akemi	[uh huh.
55	Judee	[yeah. [because he came from here he would know.
56	Jill	[uh huh.
57	Mary	uh huh.

In line 53, TF asks a closed, confirmation question to all the participants as ratified listeners. Everyone except Judee provides only a minimal response. Judee provides a minimal response in line 55 and continues to account for her response. She highlights Obama's being from Hawai'i by saying "because he came from here," which is followed by her paraphrasing of Mary's formulation (l. 50) as "he would know" (l. 55). In the end, Judee has answered her own question posed to Mary in line 1.

Excerpt 1 showed that categories are reflexively connected with one another. First, "blacks," a category that was introduced by one of the participants as a response to my question, led to a series of categories and proper nouns that included "black friends," "Barack Obama," "white and black," and "a Local boy." Second, "being raised here," a category-bound activity, led to a series of other category-bound activities that included "have so much in common," "has the ties to Hawai'i," "did all those things," "going to the beach and smoking paka," "was here long enough," "hanging out with his buddies and everything," "going surfing and doing whatevers," and finally "came from here."

I would like to make three points here; first, the four participants (Akemi, Jill, Judee, Mary) discursively constructed the meaning of being Local by assembling a series of category-bound activities, among which "being raised here" (l. 14) turned out to be the most crucial. This can be clearly seen when Judee answered her own question initially posed to Mary by responding to my last question, reformulating Mary's account about Barack Obama, and stating that "yeah. because he came from here he would know" in line 55. The participants constructed an unlikely stance object into a Local, thereby showing that Localness is not static and pre-given, but it is situated and per-formed in the particular context of a focus group session.

Second, the participants co-constructed their opinions in talk-in-interaction. While doing this, they used various epistemic stance markers (i.e., the basic linguistic resources for constructing reality and for referring to knowledge or belief in relation to some center of concern; Ochs, 1996) in order to establish the believability of Barak Obama's Localness. The use of such markers played a crucial role in the co-construction of meaning. For instance, Mary becomes assertive in lines 9–10, where she shifts her focus from talking about "blacks" to talking about Barak Obama. However, she does not become too assertive about Obama's Localness because she utters "you know" repeatedly (ll. 15, 20, 26, 29), in addition to providing other epistemic stance markers such as "I don't know" (l. 19) and "not to bring this into a political (.4) kind of situation, but" (ll. 23 and 24). She makes an assertion about Obama's life history in lines 30–33. When her assertiveness reaches a high point, Mary uses "you know" again in line 33 to conclude, using it repeatedly (ll. 43, 44, 45, 52) and responding to TF's question about Obama's ability to understand Local comedy, with a rising intonation. Her repeated use of "you know" contributes to creating a not too assertive epistemic stance towards

Obama's Localness. Mary's stancetaking is a good illustration of the fact that what one says cannot be isolated from how the speaker says it.

Third, Obama's racial heritage is part of a larger media discourse that emerged prior to and during the presidential campaign; for instance, a newspaper headline read that "Obama's Appeal to Blacks Remains an Open Question" (Fletcher 2007). Media stories such as this one include semiotic resources that circulate in society and are readily available for the focus group participants. These stories were invoked when Mary attempted to make sense of categories such as "black" or "Local" as well as of Local humor. This illustrates how the interpretation of media discourses takes place within the context of other such discourses, pointing to the significance of intertextuality.

This section has demonstrated the discursive construction of Localness or doing being Local. In the next section, the participants introduce multiple categories that stand out in sharp contrast to being Local.

4.2 White-washed

Excerpt 2 (ll. 1–53) is taken from another focus group interview that consists of six participants: Andy, H-Mom, J, Kaimana, Michi, T. As in Excerpt 1, after discussing the fourth clip, TF poses the question reproduced below in line 1.

Excerpt 2a "white washed people"
```
1   TF          who do you think (.) would dislike (.)
2               this kind of comedy.
3               (1.0)
4   Andy        m::[:::.
5   H-Mom          [anyone who doesn't understand it?
6   J                 pro[bably.
7   Kaimana              [yeah.
8   Andy                 [uh huh.
9   J           [like-
10  Michi       [>people who's ↑not from ↓here<.
11              (.4)
12  Andy        m. maybe:, like (.6) uhm (.4)
13              the ethnic people they ((comics)) are talking about
14              that aren't (.) from here?
15  Michi       yeah [maybe.
16  Kaimana          [yeah.
```

TF's question is followed by a long 1.0 second pause in line 3. Andy produces a hedging sound in line 4, and H-Mom takes the floor by providing an answer in line 5 with a rising intonation. J, Kaimana, and Andy align with her in lines 6–8. J initiates talk but immediately discontinues his utterance in line 9 when it overlaps with Michi's utterance in line 10; here, Michi provides another possible answer to TF's question, which leads to a 0.4 second pause in line 11. Andy takes up the floor in line 12 and, after a series of hedging utterances, he provides another possible answer (with rising intonation), which is built upon Michi's answer (l. 10) but is more specific about ethnicity. An indexical "here" appears twice in the above excerpt in lines 10 and 14. Its referent (i.e., "Hawai'i") is understood and is taken for granted by Michi and Andy as well as by the other participants. Both Michi and Kaimana align with Andy in lines 15 and 16, which leads to Andy's next utterance.

Excerpt 2b

```
17   Andy       that are, yeah (.) maybe like if Filipinos (.) co:me
18              and [then they hear that it's-
19   H-Mom          [<FOBs> *
20   Andy       [they could be insulted.
21   H-Mom      [HAHAHAhahaha ha.
22   Kaimana    [£yeah£.
23              like the FB[I:
24   Michi                 [sort of white [washed people,
25   Andy               or [(.2)           [like
26              ehehe.
27   Kaimana    [yeah.
28   H-Mom      [yeah.
```

Andy shows a false start and hedging, finally introducing a new category (i.e., "Filipinos") in line 17 that serves as a sub-category to a category he brought up previously (l. 13). While Andy continues his hypothesized scenario in line 18, H-Mom provides a relevant category (i.e., FOBs, which stands for "fresh off the boat" and is a pejorative term for the new immigrant population) in line 19, orienting to Andy's identification of Filipinos as a group of people who "would dislike this kind of comedy." Andy states a possible consequence in line 20, which overlaps with both H-Mom's and Kaimana's utterances in lines 21 and 22. H-Mom's laughter in line 21 follows her own utterance in line 19. Kaimana's acknowledgment token in line 22 is a response to the relevance of FOBs, so she introduces another sub-category in line 23 (i.e., FBI, which stands for "full-blooded Ilokano," a term covering both the immigrants from the Philippines and their second generation children), thereby co-constructing a collection of categories about Filipinos. The last part of Kaimana's utterance overlaps with Michi's utterance in line 24 where she brings up another category (i.e., "sort of white washed people"). It should be noted that even though there is an overlap, it is to Michi's utterance that Andy, Kaimana, and H-Mom respond in lines 26–28, acknowledging the relevance of the category to the ongoing discussion. In the next excerpt, Michi already starts to explain about her use of the category, showing an orientation to the effect of the strong language and becoming more explicit about who she considers white washed. In other words, she moves the scale of abstraction from general (i.e., "sort of white washed") to more specific (i.e., "white washed") with respect to her category work.

Excerpt 2c

29	Michi	I mean I don't wanna use the term but .h
30	Andy	[uh huh.
31	Michi	[they get they're like (.)
32		Filipino or Asian from the mainland,
33		like they're white washed.
34	Andy	[uh huh.
35	Michi	[ən ((and)) they don't understa:nd the same <reference>.
36		the ethnic jokes that we have here. .h
37	TF	uh huh.
38	Michi	because with this one (.)
39		I guess it's closer to their home culture?
40		rather than (.2) having (.) been (.)
41		assimilated to the American one?
42	Kaimana	uh huh.
43	Andy	m:.

Michi talks about the term "white washed" while other participants such as Andy, TF, and Kaimana provide minimal responses. First of all, Michi implies the effectiveness of using the term as part of a response to TF's question, even though she says she does not necessarily want to use it (l. 29). She continues to talk about those who would dislike Local comedy by identifying their ethnicity and locality and re-using the term "white washed" in line 33. She makes reference to a category-bound activity in line 35; that is, if they do not understand Local comedy, they are not Local. Michi paraphrases "the same <reference>" as "the ethnic jokes that we have here." Her use of pronouns contributes to showing the interpretive difference between non-Local and Local. She starts to account for this contrast in line 38 by referring to the kind of jokes that "we" have (l. 36). She marks the following utterance with modality (l. 39), stating that the kind of jokes under discussion are "closer to their home culture" than to mainland American culture. Michi's utterance in lines 38–41 creates two implications: (1) there is a cultural assimilation process from the home culture of immigrants to the American one and (2) Hawai'i's Local culture is somewhere in between the two points in this process. The situated meaning of being "white washed" is treated as conveying the same as "being assimilated to the mainstream culture." H-Mom continues to talk about how non-Locals would interpret Local humor.

Excerpt 2d

44	H-Mom	they would probably feel offended, and,
45	Kaimana	yeah.=
46	Michi	="↓that's [not PC:."
47	H-Mom	[kick up a ruckus.
48	Andy	[£yeah£.
49	H-Mom	[HAHAHAhahaha
50	Michi	"I'm nə ((gonna)) throw a riot now."
51	H-Mom	.h
52	Michi	m.
53	H-Mom	yeah.

In line 44, H-Mom describes the first part of a series of actions by those who would dislike the comedy under discussion. This is followed by an acknowledgment from Kaimana in line 45, which is latched with Michi's utterance in line 46, where she gives voice to those who would feel offended, as formulated by H-Mom in line 44. Michi's utterance overlaps with H-Mom's utterance (l. 47) in which she continues to describe the second part of a series of actions by the same group of people. Andy acknowledges this in line 48, which overlaps with H-Mom's laughter that marks the end of her utterance in line 49. Michi continues to give voice to the same group of people in line 50, but there is no uptake of her utterance.

Note that H-Mom (ll. 44 and 47) and Michi (ll. 46 and 50) resort to different strategies in describing the same group of people about whom I posed a question. Both of them describe category-bound activities, but while H-Mom uses the third person plural pronoun (l. 44), Michi uses the first person singular (l. 50). In addition, H-Mom's utterances are responded to by Kaimana in line 45 and by Andy in line 48 while Michi's utterances are not. This would allow for an interpretation that Michi's utterances (along with Kaimana's and Andy's) are also designed as responses to H-Mom's utterances (l. 44). In other words, Michi acknowledges H-Mom's utterances by reformulating category-bound actions (ll. 44 and 47) with a different voice and footing (ll. 46 and 50). This is how Michi aligns with H-Mom; and compared to Kaimana and Andy, Michi shows a more dialogically-complex alignment. Both Michi and H-Mom jointly construct a 'recombinant self' or a social type of those who would dislike Local humor. Being non-Local is also not pre-given, but it is situated and constructed in the particular context of a focus group session.

4.3 A different kind of humor

The third excerpt (ll. 1–83) is taken from an interview of a group of four: Craig, Kekoa, Kristy, and Sarah. Here, the interaction occurred very early in the focus group session. The participants had finished self-introductions and discussed the first question (i.e., What is the first thing that comes to mind when you hear "Local comedy?"). Following this, they were asked about their favorite comedians. After all the participants except Craig had provided their responses to the question, TF urged Craig to contribute to the ongoing discussion (line 1).

Excerpt 3a "It's a different kind of humor"

1	TF	how about you [Craig?
2	Craig	[(I know)
3		my favorite's Frank DeLima too.
4	TF:	uh huh.
5		what makes him special for you.
6	Craig	I think it's a quality that all these local,
7		(.) comedians have I think.
8		they are all endearing.
9	Sarah	[uh huh.
10	TF	[uh huh.
11	Craig	none of them ever come off uh,
12		.h <as (.) rough (.) and (.) uh>=,
13	Kekoa	=no,
14	Craig	offensive or in any way.=
15	Sarah	=or vicious,
16		(.) (harsh).
17	Craig	yeah like um (.)

Craig names Frank DeLima as his favorite comedian in line 3, followed by TF's question in line 5. He responds to this question by introducing a "quality that all these local, (.) comedians have" in lines 6–7 and specifies this quality or attribute as "endearing" in line 8. He starts to describe what Local comedians are not, by bringing in contrastive attributes (ll. 12 and 14). These attributes are co-constructed by Kekoa (l. 13) and Sarah (ll. 15 and 16) respectively, which is acknowledged by Craig (l. 17). These contrastive attributes are category-bound and associated with non-Local comedians; this becomes evident when Craig makes reference to "one guy that (.) Italian gu:y" in the next excerpt.

Excerpt 3b

18	Craig	re↑member that one guy that (.)
19		Italian gu:y,
20		it was uh (.)
21		back in the (.4)
22		early nineties,
23		.h he had the Dice,
24		>I can't remember what was his name<

25		he- uhm
26		some of these like [the mainland-
27	Sarah	[oh Andrew Dice Clay?
28		(.4)
29	Craig	Andrew Dice Clay.=
30	Kekoa	=↑Andrew ↓Dice ↑°Clay°.
31	Sarah	he was ve[ry mean.
32	Kekoa	[>he was mean<.
33	Sarah	he was [rude.
34	Craig	[uhm (.)
35		[uh (.)
36	Kristy	[mhehe

Craig makes reference to a contrastive category in lines 18–19 and throws in various pieces of relevant information including "some of these like the mainland-" in line 26. The participants jointly achieve recollecting the comedian's name in lines 27–30, adding two more category-bound attributes (ll. 31–32 and 33). Craig acknowledges Sarah's contribution in lines 34 and 35 while Kristy generates a laugh token in line 36. Craig initiates another sequence of acts involving joint name recollection in the following excerpt.

Excerpt 3c

37	Craig	what's his name uhm
38	Kristy	heh
39	Kekoa	the other one.
40		(.4)
41	Craig	the Irish gu:y [I love
42	Kekoa	[yeah.
43	Craig	he swears all the time.
44		[what was his name.
45	Kekoa	[yca:h (ya ya)
46	Craig	uhm he's at Fireman Show now,
47	Kekoa	yea[:h.
48	Craig	[Denis Leary?
49	Sarah	[m:
50	TF	[uh huh..
51	Craig	.h
52		none of the Local comedians
53		ever come off like abrasive.
54	Sarah	[uh huh.
55	TF	[uh huh.
56	Craig	they are very endearing.
57	TF	uh huh.
58	Craig	°so°.

Craig initiates a new sequence in line 37, brings in an ethnic category (l. 41) and a category-bound activity (l. 43), and completes the recollection process in line 48 when acknowledged by Sarah (l. 49) and by TF (l. 50). Craig opens up a closing sequence in line 52, further describes what Local comedians are not like by bringing in another attribute (l. 53), repeats the quality he raised earlier (l. 56), and finally closes his sequence (l. 58). Kekoa initiates discussion of another comedian in the next excerpt.

Excerpt 3d

59	Kekoa	and wasn't there one
60		like with a Parisian beret, (.2)
61		used to- (.) be really= mea:n,
62	Sarah	=oh Sam Kinison.
63	Kekoa	Sam [Kinison.
64	Craig	[£tha̱t's right£.
65	Kekoa	[Sam Kinison was very mean.
66	Craig	[that's right.
67	Sarah	yeah we don't have [that.
68	Kekoa	[yeah.
69	Sarah	*daet kain.*
70	Kekoa	↑I mean
71		they're funny probably on HB↓O, ((Home Box Office))
72		but locally I don't think
73		<↓they'll work>.
74	Craig	>it's a different kind of humor<.=
75	Kekoa	=>it's a
76		different kind of humor<.
77	TF	m:. okay. (.4)
78		good. (.2)
79		so, uhm anything to add? (.2)
80		before we move on?
81		(1.0)
82	Kekoa	no. I think we did great.
83	All	((laughter))

Kekoa starts a new sequence about a third and last non-Local comedian in line 59. The participants jointly recollect Sam Kinison in lines 62–66. Finally, Sarah makes a generalization in lines 67 and 69, and Kekoa accounts for her generalization in lines 70–73 by specifying two domains. His account is reformulated and concluded by Craig in line 74, acknowledged and repeated by Kekoa in lines 75 and 76. In short, the participants have collaboratively contrasted attributes of one type of comedians (i.e., endearing) with those of another type of comedians (i.e., rough, offensive, vicious, harsh, mean, rude, and abrasive), thereby discursively constructing two kinds of humor (i.e., Local and non-Local) that are consumed and interpreted differently in two domains (e.g., locally vs. HBO). Once again, the participants showed that the properties of Local and non-Local comedians are not pre-formed, but are per-formed in the particular context of a focus group session.

As seen from the above, the participants in the three focus groups often took matters into their own hands; for instance, in Excerpt 1 Judee initiated a question (l. 1) that led to a sequence of categorial work regarding the Localness of Barack Obama; Excerpt 2 demonstrated how the participants talked about non-Local membership categories without any interruption from me (I only posed a question (ll. 1–2) and generated a minimal response once (l. 37)); and Excerpt 3 showed that Craig, Kekoa, and Sarah jointly generated contrastive properties of Local and non-Local comedians. Furthermore, Kekoa made an evaluative comment to close up the discussion (l. 82), thereby skillfully transforming a focus group session on humor into a humorous interaction. It was evident, however, that situational identities such as 'moderator' and 'participant' contributed to creating an asymmetrical participation framework: thus, I moderated each group by means of minimal responses as acknowledgment tokens, by posing semi-structured questions, and by nominating the next respondent. Nevertheless, such situational identities were subject to change and became emerging discursive identities because each group took matters away from me and into its own hands; in this way, the focus group interview documents both asymmetry and group dynamics as its properties.

5. Discussion

The previous section presented a sequential analysis and also examined an orientation among the participants of three focus groups. Based on the above results, the present section focuses more on the latter — stancetaking towards factuality — and explores the implications of joint construction, alignment, and disalignment. Excerpt 1 revealed that the four participants (Akemi, Jill, Judee, Mary) jointly construct the meaning of being Local by assembling a series of category-bound activities among which "being raised from here" (l. 17) turned out to be the most crucial attribute. The participants treated locality, rather than ethnicity, as a defining factor for being Local, thereby jointly engineering Barack Obama as a recombinant self or a social type. It should be noted that they did not construct Obama as an individual but they treated him as a social type of Local by means of assembling the type's category-bound actions and attributes.

Moreover, when the participants depicted Obama's Localness, Judee indexed a sense of removal, too, with respect to Obama by stating "he came from here" (l. 55). In other words, Judee could have said "he is from here" instead. Both formulations imply that he has a tie with Hawai'i; however, the alternative formulation would have indicated that he is still in close proximity to the islands while the original formulation indicated that their relationship is chronotopically more distant; that is, Judee's formulation invoked another layer of the social norm about locality that being Local also demands remaining in close proximity to the islands. In any case, the participants engineered Obama as a social type of Local who can appreciate a certain type of humor, thereby treating themselves as such as well, inasmuch as they share the same attributes.

On the other hand, the meaning of being non-Local emerged in Excerpt 2, where six participants (Andy, Hawaiian Mom, J, Kaimana, Michi, T) also jointly generated category-bound activities and attributes one after another in response to my question. The specific reference to Filipinos (e.g., "Filipinos" in line 17, "FOBs" in line 19, "FBI" in line 23, and "Filipino" in line 32) can be attributed to the participants' orientation to the content of the fourth clip (See Appendix) in which comedian Augie T talks about Filipino jokes. In addition to these labels, Michi generated another category (i.e., "sort of white washed people" in line 24 and "white washed" in line 33) that contributed to creating non-Localness.

These non-Local categories were also engineered as recombinant selves that stand in chronotopical contrast to being Local. Being non-Local is in sharp contrast with being Local: while being non-Local is treated as not being from Hawai'i, being from Hawai'i is a defining component of being Local (as seen above). The participants also treated a non-Local as a social type who not only dislikes a certain kind of humor but responds emotionally by means of feeling offended and criticizing alleged violations of political correctness. The discursive deployment of these emotionally charged actions successfully established the factuality that non-Locals lack a Local sense of humor. Furthermore, it would not be an overstatement to maintain that a Local sense of humor is implied as an indication of genuine humanity.

Excerpt 3 was about comedians as stance objects; here, the four participants (Craig, Kekoa, Kristy, Sarah) displayed an orientation to broader political-economic dimensions of media circulation (i.e., local performances vs. global mediascapes), aligning with one another through jointly constructing an attribute proper to Local comics. Craig introduced the psychological attribute (i.e., "endearing") in line 8. He also described what they are not, by bringing in contrastive attributes (e.g., "rough" in line 12), which was immediately responded to by Kekoa and Sarah. The three latter participants then discussed three comedians (i.e., Andrew Dice Clay, Dennis Leary, Sam Kinison), co-constructing their attributes and adding even more attributes (e.g., "vicious"). These non-Local and mainland comedians were also identified by their alleged ethnicity, even though they apparently in the mainland are not usually identified through this kind of ethnic labeling. The use of these ethnic labels suggests that the participants were talking about the mainland comics within a crossgenre interpretive frame of Local comedy for which ethnic stereotyping plays a bigger role.

Assembling two contrastive sets of attributes as social types of Local and non-Local comedians, the participants achieved a discursive co-construction of two kinds of humor — Local and mainland — asserting that both of them can be funny in their own rights, while being different kinds of humor. By so doing, the participants not only aligned successfully with one another, but were mass-mediated with Local comedy audiences in general. This does not mean, however, that the participants disaligned completely from mainland audiences by taking the stance that they can still appreciate both kinds of humor. The constructed factuality is that Local comedy audiences can enjoy not only mainland comedy but also Local comedy — a type of comedy that is dear to these audiences — while non-Local audiences do not have that privilege. In other words, the participants dialogically constituted themselves as a Local comedy audience through talking about Local and non-Local comedians as stance objects.

In summary, the excerpts highlighted that categories are not pre-formed but per-formed in the particular context of each focus group session. Using various semiotic resources and their intertextual links with previous and relevant texts, the participants interactionally engineered Localness, non-Localness, and two kinds of humor. The participants also achieved constituting themselves dialogically as Locals through assembling these recombinant categories in the moment-by-moment flow of on-going talk.

6.   Conclusion

There has been little receptive research on media discourse; in addition, previous receptive studies were suffering from a methodological problem. I have tried to overcome this problem by taking a conversation analysis approach to focus group data. In the excerpts above, many examples showed how the participants took matters into their own hands, how they shifted from situated to discursive identities, and how their stancetaking varied (e.g., assertive vs. non-assertive), all of which would have passed unnoticed in purely content-based research.

My goal was to extend studies on intertextuality into an interactional context and contribute to recent work that examines semiotic encounters in metadiscursive talk. I selected Hawai'i comedy as a case study because this culturally specific activity is an ideologically unique site for interethnic membership categorization. I showed that the focus group participants interactionally built a collection of categories in order to interpret Local comedy, while they also talked about the mediatized performances in order to make sense of socially circulating categories of persons.

Recombinant selves or social types assembled in the specific context included a Local, a non-Local, and Local/non-local comedians. The participants also talked about two kinds of humor — Local and the mainland — and constructed the Local state of mind that can appreciate both kinds of humor; nonetheless, Local comedy remained dear to their heart. I emphasized that these categories are not fixed and pre-formed, but situated and per-formed. As my concern was about factuality, I also emphasized that interactants jointly create versions of reality in the moment-by-moment development of talk.

Moreover, the focus group participants displayed an orientation to intertextual links with past or relevant media discourses, both when they discussed Barack Obama's racial identity and when they contrasted Local with mainland humor by referring to a major cable network and invoking broader political-economic dimensions of media circulation. In all the excerpts, the participants' metaperformance talk contributed to their interpretation of the performances and reinforced the images and stereotypes they have about different social groups in the formation of Local community and humor.

Finally, in some cases it was difficult to determine what position a particular individual ended up taking. Video recording might have helped to better analyze the way relatively inactive participants reacted to the on-going discussion (through gaze and nodding). Nevertheless, I feel that my endeavors in this context may have contributed to the body of pragmatic and sociolinguistic research that takes a critical and reflexive stance by redefining the focus group as a site for interactants' active construction of identity, rather than dismissing it as inauthentic data.

Acknowledgements

I would like to thank Asif Agha, Jack Bilmes, Laurie Durand, Gavin Furukawa, Christina Higgins, Mie Hiramoto, Gabriele Kasper, Joseph Park, and Matt Prior who helped me in different stages of preparing this paper. My thanks also go to two reviewers as well as to members of the CA Data Session and Da Pidgin Coup in the University of Hawai'i at Mānoa. I am also indebted to Yujin Yaguchi, Satoshi Mori, and other members of the Hawai'i Studies Group. All the shortcomings are of course my own.

References

Agha, Asif. 2007a. Recombinant Selves in Mass Mediated Spacetime. Language & Communication, 27, 320–335.
Agha, Asif. 2007b. Language and Social Relations. Cambridge: Cambridge University Press.

Baker, Carolyn D. 2003. Ethnomethodological Analyses of Interviews. In: Inside Interviewing: New lenses, new concerns, James A. Holstein and Jaber F. Gubrium (eds), 395–412. Thousand Oaks, California: SAGE Publications.

Bauman, Richard and Briggs, Charles. 1990. Poetics and Performance as Critical Perspectives on Language and Social Life. Annual Review of Anthropology, 19, 59–88.

Blake, Fred. 1996. Interethnic Humor in Hawai'i. The Comic in the Culture: University of Hawai'i at Mānoa Summer Session 1996, 7.

Blommaert, Jan. 2005. Discourse: Key topics in sociolinguistics. Cambridge: Cambridge University Press.

Du Bois, John W. 2007. The Stance Triangle. In: Stancetaking in Discourse: Subjectivity, evaluation, interaction, Robert Englebreston (ed), 139–182. Amsterdam: John Benjamins Publishing Co.

Edwards, Derek. 1991. Categories are for Talking: On the cognitive and discursive bases of categorization. Theory & Psychology, 1, 4, 515–542.

Edwards, Derek and Stokoe, Elizabeth H. 2004. Discursive Psychology, Focus Group Interviews and Participants' Categories. British Journal of Developmental Psychology, 22, 499–507.

Fletcher, Michael A. 2007, January 25. Obama's Appeal to Blacks Remains an Open Question. Retrieved July 5, 2010 from the World Wide Web:

http://www.washingtonpost.com/wp-dyn/content/article/2007/01/24/AR2007012402032.html

Gubrium, Jaber F., and Holstein, James A. 2002. From the Individual Interview to the Interview Society. In: Handbook of Interview Research, Jaber F. Gubrium and James A. Holstein (eds), 3–32. Thousand Oaks, California: SAGE Publications.

Hutchby, Ian, and Wooffitt, Robin. 2008. Conversation Analysis (2nd ed.). Malden, Massachusetts: Polity.

Krueger, Richard A. and Casey, Mary Ann. 2009. Focus Group: A practical guide for applied research (4th ed). Los Angeles: SAGE Publications.

Morgan, David L. 2002. Focus Group Interviewing. In: Handbook of Interview Research, Jaber F. Gubrium and James A. Holstein (eds), 141–159. Thousand Oaks, California: SAGE Publications.

Myers, Greg. 2007. Enabling talk: How the facilitator shapes a focus group. Text & Talk, 27, 1, 79–105.

Ochs, Elinor. 1996. Linguistic Resources for Socializing Humanity. In: Rethinking Linguistic Relativity, John Gumperz and Stephen Levinson (eds), 407–437. Cambridge: Cambridge University Press.

Peek, Lori, and Fothergill, Alice. 2009. Using Focus Groups: Lessons from studying daycare centers, 9/11, and Hurricane Katrina. Qualitative Research, 9, 1, 31–59.

Potter, Jonathan. 1996. Representing Reality: Discourse, Rhetoric and Social Construction. London: SAGE Publications.

Potter, Jonathan, and Hepburn, Alexa. 2005. Qualitative Interviews in Psychology: Problems and Possibilities. Qualitative Research in Psychology, 2, 38–55.

Potter, Jonathan, and Hepburn, Alexa. 2008. Discursive Constructionism. In: Handbook of Constructionist Research, James A. Holstein and Jaber F. Gubrium (eds), 275–293. New York: Guildford.

Pösö, Tarja, Honkatukia, Päivi, and Nyqvist, Leo. 2008. Focus Groups and the Study of Violence. Qualitative Research, 8, 1, 73–89.

Puchta, Claudia, and Potter, Jonathan. 2004. Focus Group Practice. London: SAGE Publications.

Roulston, Kathryn. 2006. Close Encounters of the 'CA' Kind: A review of literature analyzing talk in research interviews. Qualitative Research, 6, 535–554.

Sacks, Harvey. 1979. Hotrodder: A revolutionary category. In: Everyday Language: Studies in ethnomethodology, George Psathas (ed), 7–14. Hillsdale, New Jersey: Lawrence Erlbaum Associates.

Spitulnik, Debra. 2001. The Social Circulation of Media Discourse and the Mediation of Communities. In: Linguistic Anthropology: A reader, Alessandro Duranti (ed), 95–118. Oxford: Blackwell Publishing.

Warren, Carol A. B. 2002. Qualitative Interviewing. In: Handbook of Interview Research, Jaber F. Gubrium and James A. Holstein (eds), 83–101. Thousand Oaks, California: SAGE Publications.

Wilkinson, Sue. 2004. Focus Group Research. In: Qualitative Research (2nd ed), David Silverman (ed), 177–199. London: SAGE Publications.

Wilkinson, Sue. 2008. Analyzing Interaction in Focus Groups. In: Talk and Interaction in Social Research Methods, Paul Drew, Geoffrey. Raymond, and Darin Weinberg (eds), 50–62. London: SAGE Publications.

Yuen, Mike. 1998, July 24. No joke: Bu La'ia likely to be disqualified as candidate for governor — again. Honolulu Star-Bulletin. Retrieved July 4, 2010 from the World Wide Web: http://archives.starbulletin.com/1998/07/24/news/story8.html

Zimmerman, Don H. 1998. Identity, Context and Interaction. In: Identities in Talk, Charles Antaki and Sue Widdicombe (eds), 87–106. London: SAGE Publications.

Transcription conventions

.	Falling intonation		_	Emphasis
,	Continuing contour		:	Sound stretching
?	Questioning intonation		CAPS	Louder than surrounding talk
↑↓	Prominent rising or falling intonation		< >	Slower than surrounding talk
(1.0)	Pause of about 1 second		> <	Quicker than surrounding talk
(.2)	Pause of about 0.2 second		£ £	Laughing voice
(.)	Micro pause		° °	Quieter than surrounding talk
h/.h	Breathing (out breath / in breath)		=	Latching
[	Overlap		*	Unable to transcribe
" "	Reported speech		( )	Unsure transcription
-	Abrupt cut-off		(( ))	Other details

Appendix

Augie T is one of the most popular comedians in Hawai'i. I observed and audio-recorded his comedy show at a hotel in Honolulu in 2008. The show was held every Friday evening. The room was packed with approximately 70–80 people of various ages, most of whom seemed to be Local residents. He talks about a stereotypical cultural practice of those of Filipino descent below. For reasons of space, what follows is only the first half of a four minute long clip:

Clip "Don't get judgmental. Relax. It's fun. It's comedy!"

1	AT	*nating* ((nothing)) to complain (.)
2		having a good time.
3		it's <u>us</u> to complain.
4		it's <u>us</u> to get judgmental.
5	Woman	hahaha
6	AT	*don* get judgmen↑tal (.) rela:x (.) it's fun (.) it's comedy.
7	Woman	haha
8	AT	you know who get mad? (.)
9		the filipinos always get mad at me at the beginning.
10		when I did comedy (.) you know (.)
11		I guess they *neva* know I was filipino in the [beginning.
12	Aud	[hahahahahahaha
13	AT	I guess when you mix (.) portuguese and filipinos
14		you turn mexican
15	Aud	hahahahahaha
16	AT	I *don* know.
17		but I used to like when we going eat food,
18		come here (.) come here (.) come here (1.0) come here.
19		what do you mean (fricking) pilipino *jo*? ((joke))
20	Aud	hahahahahahahaha
21	AT	you stupid (if) p<u>u:</u>nny you got pilipino (jok).
22	Aud	hahahahaha
23	AT	it's not pu:nny.
24		what do you mean that ** pilipino *jok*?
25		(if) you stupid. you ST<u>U:</u>PID.
26		it's not punny.
27		(and this is) <u>fu</u>nny (.) it's <u>fu</u>nny. why are you all get mad?
28	Aud	hahahahaha
29	AT	you know what?
30		and we <*s<u>o:</u>* n<u>u</u>mb> to it, you know, we *so:* numb (.)
31		we live in hawaii.
32		guess what? (.)
33		we *gon* talk about ethnic things (.)
34		all right? (.)
35		and you know,
36		uh it's funny how (.) the news *chraiz* ((tries)) to be (.) pee.
37		see. but *ha:d* ((hard)) when you live in hawaii
38		and when you get (um) dog (.) getting eaten at the golf course.
39	Aud	hahahahahahaha
40	AT	*** (.) *** (1.5)
41		((To a group of people from the mainland who are sitting to his
42		left))

43		my friends from the mainland (.)
44		<a do:g (.) was taken from a golf cours(h)e (.) and eaten> (.)
45		that's right (.) *ya ya ya*
46		o: lunch (.) right *dea* (.)
47	Aud	hahahahaha
48	AT	but (.5) correct me if I'm wrong. (.5)
49		*okei?* (.5)
50		took the news three weeks before they (even) identify (.) who
51		did *um.*
52	Aud	hahahahaha
53	AT	£you know why£? huh?
54		because that's °very sensitive° (.5)
55	Aud	hahahahaha
56	AT	haha (.) as soon as it happened (.)
57		what happened (.)
58		while we all (say) (.)
59		a̲: (.) a: (.) uh↑ somebody (leave) one dog at *da* golf ↓course
60	Aud	((light laughter))
61	AT	<ho̲:s da̲mn to̲ngans ya?>
62	Aud	hahahahahahaha
63	AT	(cause someone) did it right? ******
64		that's why (you) da̲mn to̲ngans.
65		*no̲:.*
66		*so:* funny how they did it right?
67		>it said< (.)
68		<°u:h dog was taken (.) from the (.) golf cou:rse (.) by two̲:
69		maintenance workers°>.
70	Aud	hahahahahahaha
71	AT	and then the the £follow(h)ing * listen£ (.)
72		<°from *wai pa:* [*hu:*°>
73	Aud	[hahahahahahaha
74	AT	and they showed these two filip(h)i(h)n(h)o(h) g(h)u(h)y(h)s
75		(over here).
76		£stu:pi̲d, we already kno̲:w£.
77	Aud	hahahahahahaha
78	AT	(we kno:w and) we *no:* ((know)) filipinos like eat do:gs.
79		[*jas* sa̲y it.
80	Aud	[hahahahahahaha
81	AT	it's oka:y. we understa̲:nd. (.) right?
82		<we no̲: alre̲a:↑dy>

Performing the 'lifeworld' in public education campaigns

Media interdiscursivity and social governance

Michelle M. Lazar
National University of Singapore

In Singapore, top down public education campaigns have long been a mode of governance by which the conduct of citizens is constantly regulated. This article examines how in two fairly recent campaigns, a new approach to campaign communication is used that involves media interdiscursivity, viz., the mixing of discourses and genres in which the media constitute a significant element. The present approach involves the appropriation of a popular local television character, 'Phua Chu Kang', in order to address the public through educational rap music videos.

Media interdiscursivity is based on an attempt to engage the public via a discourse of the 'lifeworld'. The present article analyzes the 'lifeworld' discourse in terms of a combination of two processes, 'informalization' (the use of informal and conversational modes of address) and 'communitization' (the semiotic construction of a community of people). The dual processes are examined and discussed in relation to the choice of Phua Chu Kang as an 'ordinary' and almost 'real' person, including his informal register and speech style; his use of Singlish; and his construction of 'community'. The presence of Singlish, in particular, is interesting because (despite the official disdain for the language) it is included as part of PCK's public performance of the lifeworld. The article concludes by considering this form of media interdiscursivity as the government's shrewd way of achieving its social governance goals.

1. Introduction

If the work of government, as Foucault asserted, is "the conduct of conduct" (Gordon 1987:296), then public education campaigns are a key mode of governance in Singapore by which the conduct of citizens is constantly regulated. Campaigns, in fact, are so prevalent in Singapore that they have become a hallmark of social life in the city-state for more than forty years. Over time, a challenge for the ruling government has been to offset the public's inevitable campaign fatigue by continuously updating its campaign approaches, keeping them fresh, relevant and engaging, in order to sustain the public's receptivity of the messages. One approach appears to have involved a shift from using the disembodied institutional voice of the government to adopting an embodied lifeworld voice of the public.

In this article, I examine a fairly recent strategy employed, a few years apart, in two separate campaigns of using a popular local television character to address the public, as someone belonging to the lifeworld. The character in question is 'Phua Chu Kang', the lead character in a hugely popular 1990s situation comedy, titled after him *Phua Chu Kang Pte. Ltd.* 'Phua Chu Kang', played by actor Gurmit Singh, of mixed Indian-Chinese parentage, represents a Chinese renovations contractor with big curly hair, a distinctive facial mole, and wearing his trademark yellow Wellington boots. 'PCK', as he became affectionately known, was a funny and likeable character, as an average person, exhibiting common Singaporean foibles, and speaking Singlish — the colloquial variety of English spoken by the locals. Given the government's official stand against Singlish as a 'corrupt' form of English that hinders Singaporeans in using 'proper' English, the selection of PCK, and hence Singlish — the language associated with PCK and his rise to fame — in national public education campaigns is a surprising move. PCK was first used by the government to address Singaporeans via a rap music video in a public health campaign, at the height of the SARS (Severe Acute Respiratory Syndrome) outbreak, in 2003. Six years later, in 2009, PCK was featured once again in another rap music video to promote a different campaign, namely, to encourage courteous behavior on local public transportation.

This article aims to show how PCK is used in both campaigns to perform the 'lifeworld' through the combined processes of *informalization* (Featherstone 1991; Fairclough 1992, 1997) — the use of informal, conversational-like discourse, and *communitization* (Lazar 2003) — the semiotic construction of a community of people. The analysis of the data will reveal how the dual processes of 'lifeworld' construction are enacted in a number of ways: the choice of the PCK character for his ordinariness and almost 'real' personhood status; PCK's informal register and speech-style; the use of Singlish; and the enactment of 'community'. The aim of the study, ultimately, is to understand the efficacy (at least from the government's point of view) of using this form of media interdiscursivity for the purpose of social governance.

In what follows, a description of national campaigns as a mode of social governance is provided, followed by the role of 'media interdiscursivity' (viz., hybridity involving the media) in the discourse of social governance. I then analyze how the 'lifeworld' is enacted through the dual processes of informalization and communitization. The article concludes by identifying some of the implications that such media interdiscursivity may have for the governance of Singaporeans.

2. National campaigns and social governance

National campaigns are a communicational technology of planned social change. They are organized and sustained communicational strategies of social engineering, where the aim is to steer target groups towards preferred (or away from dispreferred) attitudes, values, habits and lifestyles. Insofar as they are intended to ultimately benefit individuals and are for the 'collective good', public education campaigns can be said to constitute a form of benign social control.

Using public campaigns to gear people towards social change is not an uncommon practice around the world, and has been initiated by governments as well as by non-governmental lobby and interest groups, on a wide range of issues such as population control, environmental protection, health and social awareness, and choice of language variety and standards of language usage. What makes Singapore distinctive is the extent to which public campaigns permeate all aspects of its social fabric, earning it the reputation as a 'campaign city' or 'campaign country' (Lazar 2000). In a year, an average of ten national public campaigns is in operation. Some run throughout the year, while others last for shorter durations: a few months or weeks of the year, or even one day. Since self-government began in 1959, Singaporeans have witnessed a wide array of campaigns. The earlier campaigns typically proscribed and punished (through fines and other disincentives) dispreferred practices such as littering, spitting in public places, water wastage, drug abuse, and having 'too many' children per household. Later drives adopted a more persuasive (rather than punishing) approach in advocating particular socially and economically desirable practices. These include the cultivation of courtesy and kindness; the promotion of particular language varieties and standards (Mandarin amongst the Chinese, and 'good English' among all Singaporeans); increasing workers' economic productivity; maintaining a healthy lifestyle; keeping the environment 'clean and green'; and even finding romance, getting married and — in a reversal of an earlier population policy[1] — having ('three or more') children per household.

If Singapore is (in) a state of perpetual campaigns, it is because the national campaigns represent a predominant mode of governance by the political leadership. Since the ruling government, the People's Action Party (PAP), came to power 51 years ago, national campaigns have been used regularly as a government

---

1. From 1972, the government implemented a Family Planning campaign that discouraged married couples from having more than two children. However, by the mid-1980s, the government discovered that births had fallen drastically to below national replacement levels, and introduced a new population policy, and concomitantly, a new Family Life campaign in 1990, which encouraged couples to have larger families. For details of the latter campaign, see Lazar 2000.

technology of social control and change. Fitting the description of a 'society of control' (Rose 1996), Singapore's campaigns deal with the implementation of a variety of government initiatives that seek to constantly monitor and (re)shape almost every aspect of Singaporeans' conduct. Public campaigns strive to cultivate a socially regulated, compliant and useful citizenry, in a country without natural resources except its (multi-ethnic) people.

Although campaigns have been a constant feature of governance by the PAP, the design and implementation of the campaigns have not remained the same. Rather, they have changed over the decades, responding to citizens' fatigue of blatant campaign methods and to the changing expectations of the younger generation. Further, it is not a coincidence that notable changes in the style of communication have co-occurred with shifts in the political field of government itself, viz., differences in the style of governance practiced by Singapore's first Prime Minister, Lee Kuan Yew (1959–1990), and his successors, Goh Chok Tong (1990–2004) and Lee Hsien Loong, the present Prime Minister (2004-to date). Whereas the first Lee, renowned as the 'Father of Independent Singapore', maintained tight social control over the country through a top-down, authoritarian and paternalistic leadership style, Goh and the younger Lee (Lee Kuan Yew's son), while maintaining continuity, have provided a 'softer', more mediated style of leadership.

This article focuses on the design and implementation of two separate national public education campaigns in recent years: a one-time health campaign launched in 2003; and the 2009–2010 annual courtesy campaigns. The 2003 health campaign concerned the SARS pandemic, which had directly impacted upon Singapore both in terms of the economy (businesses, especially in the tourism and transport-related sectors had been severely hit (Lim et.al 2003)), and numbers of lives affected (238 reported cases of SARS and 33 fatalities (Leong et.al 2006)). The government ran an extensive public education campaign that reminded Singaporeans to take precautionary steps against infection, like washing hands thoroughly with soap, refraining from travel to SARS-affected countries, and practicing general civic responsibility. These were communicated via numerous conventional public information avenues such as posters, booklets, bulletins, websites and television. Even a special SARS television channel was launched during the crisis period, dedicated to providing daily updates. The government's comprehensive communication strategy, described as "finely calibrated to reach out to the maximum number of people" (Menon 2006), earned international commendation. The World Health Organization (WHO), in fact, sought Singapore's support in 2004 to host the first WHO Expert Consultation on Outbreak Communication, and in his welcome address, the Director-General of WHO had noted,

There are few places that have demonstrated so clearly that the principles of out-break communication work just as well in Asia as anywhere else, perhaps even better. The risk communications Singapore used during the SARS outbreak won praise worldwide [...]. (reported in Menon 2006)

As part of the government's vigorous campaign efforts, the Ministry of Health and the Health Promotion Board collaborated with Channel 5, the existing local English-medium television channel, to co-produce what was called the 'SAR-Vi-vor Rap', an MTV-style rap music video, which reminded Singaporeans to observe precautionary measures against the disease. The full version of the video, which was four minutes long, was first screened on Channel 5 and TV Mobile (television on public buses)[2] on 12 June 2003, followed by shorter versions in the subsequent weeks. A music CD was released on 1 July 2003, which then was available at music stores island-wide.

Unlike the SARS campaign that was set up and ran only for the duration of the critical period in 2003, the National Courtesy Campaign is one of the longest run-ning, annual campaigns in Singapore. Its goal has been to change boorish habits of Singaporeans and (re-)create a society of people who are more courteous and gracious towards others, especially strangers. The idea was originally hatched on a modest scale by the local tourism board that wanted to inculcate in Singaporeans a friendlier and courteous disposition towards tourists in order to boost the tourist trade. In 1979, former Prime Minister Lee Kuan Yew extended the idea, launching a national campaign that would apply to interactions amongst all Singaporeans in all sectors of social life. Considered the hallmark of a truly civilized society, Lee reasoned, courtesy and graciousness were a necessary complement to the coun-try's accelerating economic progress (MITA, 1999). After 1993, the government bowed out of the central administration of the campaign, in its stead setting up a Courtesy Council, comprising members from the private sector. However, even though the government is no longer the formal organizer, the government keeps abreast of the campaign's development; its presence is keenly felt, for example, through VIP addresses by government ministers at the annual campaign launches. In the early 1990s, too, the campaign began to actively identify and target specific communities of people instead of addressing the public generally. Over the years, the specific communities targeted with specific messages of courtesy have includ-ed school children, retailers, employers and employees, Singaporeans working and

---

2. TV Mobile was a subsidiary of MediaCorp TV, Singapore's only television station. TV Mo-bile pioneered the use of Digital Video Broadcast technology to deliver television programmes (entertainment and real-time news) to commuters on public buses. MediaCorp TV discontin-ued TV Mobile on 1 January 2010 upon the expiry of its agreement with Singapore Bus Services Transit. (http://en.wikiperdia.org/wiki/TVMobile)

studying abroad, internet and mobile phone users, motorists, and commuters using public transportation. The long term objective was eventually to transform all sectors of Singapore society to become 'naturally' courteous (Wong, 1993, quoted in MITA, 1999: 104; Hu, 1998).

The present study focuses on the 2009–2010 drive that targeted users of public transportation. Lack of courtesy in the domain of public transportation has been a perennial concern, and has led to the intensification of campaign efforts in this area over the years. In the 1999–2003 period, the campaign was more broadly conceived to include the whole of the public road and transportation field. The aim was to tackle all sorts of anti-social behavior such as motorists changing lanes suddenly and without signaling, train and bus commuters hogging seats and crowding at doorways, and the boorishness of drivers in general. Apart from such factors as the city-state's dense population, the scarcity of land, and the heavy traffic on existing roads, especially during peak hours, the lack of consideration for others springs from a 'kiasu' attitude amongst Singaporeans (*kiasu* is a Hokkien term meaning 'the fear of losing out to others, which fosters a me-first mentality.') As the Minister for Transport, Yeo Cheow Tong, had remarked, "Even a short journey can turn into a nightmare when people are rude and aggressive to each other" (*The Straits Times*, 17 July 1999). He urged people to practice simple acts of courtesy like giving way to fellow motorists, and for commuters to move to the rear or middle of buses and trains, and give up seats to those in greater need. In the present 2009–2010 drive, the focus is directed specifically on the behavior of commuters on public buses and the mass rapid transit (MRT) trains, reminding them to be considerate towards fellow commuters. Similar to the SAR-Vivor Rap, a courtesy-themed music video titled 'A happy journey starts like that!' was produced, and is being played from time to time on board the MRT trains. The doors of the trains and the glass partitions next to seats reserved for the aged or the disabled carry courtesy messages on large cut-out stickers. Public buses, too, have courtesy messages on posters displayed behind the drivers' seat.

In both the SARS and courtesy music videos (as well as the courtesy stickers and posters on board the buses and trains), PCK, the character from the local sitcom, played a central role. In the music videos, PCK was the rap performer, while the stickers and posters on trains and buses portrayed him and his reel wife, Rosie Phua. The next section outlines the role of media interdiscursivity in national campaigns, specifically in terms of using a television character to address public education messages.

3.   The role of media interdiscursivity in social governance

Bakhtin (1986) originally introduced the idea of 'intertextuality' to refer to the animation of elements of one or more discourses within another discourse. Fairclough (1992, 1997) categorized intertextuality into two kinds: 'manifest intertextuality', which refers to bits of previous texts incorporated into the present text — his 'discourse representation' is an example of this; and 'interdiscursivity', which involves the mixing of discourses and genres, such as when corporate promotional discourse is found in brochures typically designed by educational institutions. The nature of interdiscursivity may be sequential (with different discourse types alternating within a text); embedded (where one discourse type is embedded within another); or hybridized (where discourse types are enmeshed in a more complex and less distinguishable manner; see van Leeuwen 1987; Tolson 1991; Fairclough 1992).

'Media interdiscursivity', in this article, refers to the mixing of discourses involving the media in some form; the present focus is on how a fictional character from the media is appropriated and put to 'work' within the domain of social governance. The mixing of discourses from the domains of the media and governance, in the service of furthering government imperatives is not surprising in view of government-media relations in Singapore. In one of several interviews about the role of mainstream media in Singapore, Mr. Lee Kuan Yew (then Senior Minister) (*The other Side of the Tube*, 2003) explained the media's role as fundamentally serving the goal of 'nation-building' — a concept that has come to be equated specifically with pro-government initiatives. According to Lee, ever since the early years of PAP rule, television has been regarded as "a way of guiding people along the path we wanted to go." The instrumental function of television remains today; Lee outlined the need for local television stations to be "able to hold their viewership so that when the government needs to talk, the Prime Minister has to talk directly to the people, there is a local station that has a regular viewership, and he can get his message across." Thus, even though the media were privatized more than a decade ago, the parameters of the media's functions continue to be spelled out by the government.[3]

Not only are the information media in Singapore manifestly pro-nation/pro-government: the entertainment media are, too. Neither does media interdiscursivity in terms of drawing upon television characters to address national/government concerns represent a novel practice. With the growth in production of local situation comedies in the 1990s, this media genre had become to be used, sometimes overtly, as an avenue for public education. For example, an award-winning sitcom,

---

3. The sole shareholder of MediaCorp Singapore is Temasek Holdings, which is headed by the wife of PM Lee Hsien Loong.

Under One Roof (1994–2003), which had as its premise the everyday concerns of an average Singaporean (Chinese) family living in public housing, was used to promote 'Total Defence', a new initiative by the government at the time. Conceptualized as comprising five aspects of defence — military, civil, economic, social, and psychological — the 'Total Defence' campaign sought to educate Singaporeans on the different things that can be done every day in every sector of society in order to strengthen the resilience of the nation. In line with the campaign efforts, the Ministry of Defence commissioned an *Under One Roof Total Defence* special in February 2001, in which one episode was specifically scripted to convey the message of how the average Singaporean family has a part to play in Total Defence. The patriarch of the 'reel family', Tan Ah Teck, was the key character chosen to drive home this message to his family (and television viewers), viz., that ensuring the country's security was every Singaporean's responsibility. He did this through story-telling ("This reminds me of a story. A long time ago, in the Southern province of China..."); this technique was characteristic of Tan Ah Teck, who would sagely deliver the lesson embodied in each week's episode.

In the present study, a character from another local sitcom, *Phua Chu Kang Pte Ltd.* (1997–2007), which was one of the highest rated shows in Singapore's television history, has been chosen to convey institutional messages. However, the type of media interdiscursivity here is quite different from that practiced in the earlier case. Whereas in the example of *Under One Roof*, the institutional message was threaded into the content of the existing sitcom genre, in the case of *Phua Chu Kang Pte. Ltd.*, there is a shift in frame, which involves the character from the sitcom stepping out from the remit of the entertainment genre to specifically perform the public education role. And the interdiscursivity in this case is even more complex: the public education discourse itself (pertaining, separately, to SARS and courtesy) gets re-presented in another entertainment format, namely, the genre of popular music videos. The 'person' of PCK, constitutes the focal point through which this complex interdiscursivity is played out. Drawing on Bakhtin's (1986) notion of 'double-voicing', the term 'speaker interdiscursivity' (or 'speaker hybridity') may be used to refer to the process where a speaker (or character) carrying stereotypical attributes associated with one domain or genre crosses over into another domain, and in so doing, simultaneously performs multiple identities and functions.

Speaker interdiscursivity comprises a communicative event in which 'layers of interaction' are involved beyond the immediate interactional setting. For example, in terms of audience design, a layer of interaction dealing with the immediate setting of a television studio interview may be embedded within another layer of interaction involving live and/or mass audiences (Bell 1991). Goffman (1981) noted that communicators change 'footing' (as kinds of speakers and hearers), as they traverse the layers of interaction. In the case of the SARS and courtesy educational music videos, PCK moves away from interacting with other characters within the sitcom world, to directly addressing a cross-section of 'Singaporeans' featured in the video and the mass home audience. Unlike the *Under One Roof* case, where the home audience of the public education message were only 'overhearers' (third persons, not ratified as listeners, but expected to be listening in), the campaigns involving PCK show a shift in footing whereby the audiences switch from being 'overhearers' to 'addressees' (the target audience who are directly addressed in second person). In other words, they are not viewers of an entertainment program (sitcom), who happen to receive the public education messages; rather, they are positioned from the outset as recipients of the public education messages which happen to be transmitted via an entertainment mode (music video).

In terms of communicator roles, in the music videos PCK performs as himself (the 'reel' character) as well as being a spokesperson for the relevant institutions. Using Goffman's categories of 'principal' (originator of the message whose position is expressed) and 'animator' (a physical sounding box verbatim relaying a message) to refer to the government/Courtesy Council and PCK, respectively, is therefore not straightforward. Although PCK is speaking on behalf of the government and the Courtesy Council, he is not strictly an animator, as there is a shift away from an institutional voice to that of the lifeworld. In some instances, PCK also assumes a pseudo-principal role in communication. As evident from the SAR-Vivor rap lyrics, sometimes directives are represented as personally issued by him: "PCK say don't play, play... But we can fight this, you and me" and "But listen to me and we'll be OK lah."

The use of media interdiscursivity in having a popular television character promote social governance depends for its leverage on lifeworld appeal. The next section will outline how the lifeworld is simultaneously performed and engaged through the character of Phua Chu Kang.

4.   Performing the lifeworld in the SARS and courtesy campaigns

In a 2003 interview, former Prime Minister Lee Kuan Yew conceded the need to keep up with the times in order to engage a contemporary audience: "It's a different world and a different generation. You have to go along with the fashions and tastes, in what the contemporary world understands to be attractive" (*The Other Side of the Tube*, 2003). Lee was speaking of the need of the mainstream media in Singapore to reinvent themselves so as to stay relevant in the contemporary context, but the same can be said of campaign presentations as well. The use of PCK within the SARS and Courtesy national campaigns, I argue, is one way of how 'reinventing' is done. Rather than adopt an impersonal, institutional voice, using the character of PCK allows the campaign messages to be communicated personally through the voice of the lifeworld.

My study shows how the lifeworld gets performed by PCK through the combined processes of 'informalization' and 'communitization'. 'Informalization' involves the injection of informal modes of address into public discourses that are not typically informal in nature (Featherstone 1991; Fairclough 1992). It simulates ordinary, personal and conversational communication between known participants and is interactionally engaging. 'Communitization' involves addressing an audience as members of a shared community. In accordance with Anderson's (1983/2006) concept of 'imagined' community, a community does not have an *a priori* existence, but is invoked and created through acts of semiotic mediation. The concept of 'community', being laden with connotations of inclusiveness, cohesiveness and belonging, all of which traditionally resonate with the lifeworld, provides also, in Rose's (1996) terms, access to a new means of governing individual and collective life. In what follows, I shall consider the ways in which the lifeworld via the two combined processes is performed by PCK in the SARS and Courtesy music videos. (The lyrics of the songs may be found in the Appendix.)

4.1 The ordinariness and quasi-personhood status of PCK

The first thing to consider is why PCK (rather than some other television character) was repeatedly chosen to perform the lifeworld in the public education campaigns. Of all the characters in Singapore's television history, PCK stands out as an enormously popular figure with a large fan base and instant and unique 'brand' recognition amongst Singaporean viewers. He is easily recognizable for his comic appearance and mannerisms: big, permed curly hair; a long fingernail on his pinky; a distinctive mole on his cheek; he wears his shirt half-tucked out and his trouser legs stuffed into yellow workman boots. He also has distinctive mannerisms in the way he walks, talks, sits, stands and laughs and displays stereotypical Singaporean traits, such as being materialistic and 'kiasu'. He represents an 'ordinary' person, lowly-educated and of humble beginnings, who thanks to hard work and a shrewd business sense now owns a successful renovations company ("Phua Chu Kang Pte. Ltd."). Moreover, PCK is characteristically down-to-earth, unpretentious, straight-talking, and humorous, all of which makes him an immensely likeable character. PCK is someone whom the average Singaporean viewer can identify with in each episode, not only for the way PCK navigates his work roles (as the boss of his contractor company, with his fair share of allies and competitors) but also in his family roles (as husband, elder brother, brother-in-law, son and uncle). His appeal can be seen from the description offered by former Prime Minister Goh Chok Tong, who had noted how PCK's popularity had inadvertent repercussions on the declining standards of English spoken by his fans (more on language standards below):

> ...students may think that it is acceptable and even fashionable to speak like Phua Chu Kang. He is on national TV and a likeable, ordinary person. The only character who tries to speak proper English is Phua Chu Kang's sister-in-law, Margaret, and she is a snob. Nobody wants to be a snob. So in trying to imitate life, Phua Chu Kang has made the teaching of proper English [in schools] more difficult. (Goh, 1999)

PCK's popularity has led him to cross over into domains and genres and, in so doing, he seems to have acquired quasi-personhood status, being treated as a person in his own right. Not only has PCK endorsed numerous commercial products as a celebrity spokesperson, he also represented Singaporeans as a participant in the popular US reality TV series, *Amazing Race*. Perhaps, most strikingly, even the former Prime Minister referred to PCK as if he were a 'real' person with an actual linguistic trajectory and personal volition.[4] In the same 1999 address to the nation, Goh Chok Tong said:

> I asked TCS [Television Corporation of Singapore] why Phua Chu Kang's English is so poor. They told me that Phua Chu Kang started off speaking quite good English, but as time passed he forgot what he learnt in school, and his English went from bad to worse. I therefore asked TCS to try persuading Phua Chu Kang to attend NTUC's BEST classes,[5] to improve his English. TCS replied that they have spoken to Phua Chu Kang, and he has agreed to enroll himself for the next BEST programme, starting in a month's time. If Phua Chu Kang can improve himself, surely so can the rest of us.

PCK thus occupies a liminal position between the fictitious and the 'real'; and is closer to the lived lifeworld and part of the community than any other screen character.

4.2 PCK's register and speech style

Part of the lifeworld experience is in the use of the informal, spoken register which constitutes people's everyday, ordinary, personal interaction. PCK does not move

---

4. Treating PCK as 'real' in spite of his fictional status recalls the example of Matigari, the protagonist in Ngugi wa Thiongo's fictional piece *Matigari*. A warrant was issued for the arrest of a 'Mr. Matigari' in Kenya after the book was published, since the novel revealed the protagonist's strong anti-government sentiments. I am grateful to one of the anonymous reviewers for pointing out this example.

5. This refers to a basic literacy program for adults, organized by Singapore's National Trade Union Congress.

between registers in his personal interactions and in his job capacity as a contractor, and is known, characteristically, to speak in a single (informal) register, regardless of the occasion. The informality of the music video lyrics in the two campaigns, therefore, is entirely in keeping with this character. The informal, conversational style of communication (referred to by Fairclough (1992) as 'conversationalisation') is cued discursively in the lyrics in a number of ways. One way is through using vocative markers to get the addressees' attention:

(1)   *Hey*, you over there. (Courtesy lyrics)

(2)   *Hey*, if you <u>kena</u> Home Quarantine. (SARS lyrics)

(3)   *Eh*, why you wish to catch that plane? (SARS lyrics)

Contracted forms, being indexical of informal language use, are commonly found in both sets of data. In (4) and (5), the main verb ('is', 'are') as well as the negative polarity marker ('not') are contracted. (6) is an instance of an elliptical expression, a form of clausal contraction which leaves parts of the clause implicit.

(4)   *There's* space behind, *can't* you see? (Courtesy lyrics)

(5)   If *you're* sick, *don't* go to work. (SARS lyrics)

(6)   just got on? (Courtesy lyrics)

Informality is also cued through colloquial vocabulary and expressions such as:

(7)   this *stupid* SARS (SARS lyrics)

(8)   If you're sick, don't go to work. Even if your boss is a *jerk*. (SARS lyrics)

(9)   Can't SARS me *baby*, and I don't mean maybe. (SARS lyrics)

(10) But listen to me and we'll be *OK* <u>lah</u>. (SARS lyrics)

PCK's linguistic repertoire is not only characterized by an informal register; its distinctive speech style, too, reflects PCK's character. For example, PCK's speech can be rather brusque and direct, expressing his unrefined and also rather candid personality. Thus, even though in his series of instructions in (11) through (14) PCK sounds bossy, nagging, and scolding, and sometimes wags his index finger disapprovingly at the viewers, such gestures are not intended to be rude or patronizing, as they are in line with PCK's personality. Besides, the response-demanding utterances contribute to the conversational character of the lifeworld interaction.

(11) Don't cut queue, don't you dare. Wait your turn to board the train. (Courtesy lyrics)

(12) before you go in, let them out. Before you sit, look around. Just got on? Move to the back. (Courtesy lyrics)

(13) Everyone listen. Be gracious. (Courtesy lyrics)

(14) Cover your mouth if you cough or sneeze. You think everyone want [sic] to catch your disease? (SARS lyrics)

In a few instances (see 15 and 16), PCK's downright face-threatening lyrics are potentially offensive and appear indeed paradoxical in a campaign promoting courteous behavior. Yet, viewed in the context of PCK's television personality, his flouting of the politeness maxims is not out of sync with his character. In fact, speaking bluntly in this manner signals social proximity with fellow Singaporeans — compare Brown and Levinson's (1987) characterization of such speakers who may, for similar reasons, dispense with politeness strategies, opting instead to go bald-on-record. Other mitigating circumstances likewise render the baldness of these statements acceptable. In (15), the utterance is addressed to a character in the video (not the viewer); that individual is represented as an inconsiderate member of the community, who deserves rightfully to be chastised (also the chide, "I give you a kick!", is prefaced apologetically with "Excuse me"). While in example (16) the reiteration of the directive signals impatience and exasperation with the viewers, it is also one of PCK's famous catchphrases from the sitcom. The intertextual reference afforded by the expression, thus, removes its deprecatory sting in the context of the lyrics.

(15) Hey you, pretending to sleep. Nodding and drooling in the reserved seat. Not pregnant, old or really in need. Excuse me, while I give you a kick! (Courtesy lyrics)

(16) just use your brain, use your brain, use your braaainnnn. (SARS lyrics)

As much as PCK's speech style is recognizably direct, it is also peppered with a lot of humor, which has endeared him to viewers. (17) to (21) are examples of linguistic humor in the SARS music video, and reflect funny-man PCK. The humor here is based on clever phonological twists (17 and 18), word coinages (19 and 20), and a creative turn of phrase for rhythmic effect (21):

(17) be safe, not *SAR-y*

(18) Then you can be a *SAR-vivor*

(19) See the same one [doctor], don't be a *doc-hopper*.

(20) Don't do things and be a *'regret-ter'*

(21) SARS is the virus that *I just want to minus*

4.3 The use of Singlish

Related to PCK's speech style and informal register is his use of Singlish, a colloquial variety of Singapore English. The choice of Singlish contributed to the believability of his character in the sitcom, as a lowly-educated contractor speaking basilectal English. At the same time, as Singlish is the language variety associated with informal, everyday community life in Singapore, speaking Singlish so naturally on national television instantly added to PCK's charm. As earlier indicated in the comments by former Prime Minister Goh Chok Tong in his 1999 national address, PCK's use of Singlish and his inadvertent popularizing of it amongst his fans were frowned upon by the government, which subsequently launched another national campaign, called the Speak Good English Movement (SGEM), to monitor the English standards of Singaporeans.

Even before SGEM was launched in April 2000, the government showed its long-standing aversion to Singlish by privileging Standard Singapore English (SSE) as the only allowable variety of English for Singaporeans. This attitude was born out of the government's instrumentalist language ideology that stressed the benefits of promoting 'standard English': it is internationally intelligible, it is the language of science and technology, and it provides a ticket to an effective competition in the global economy. From a pragmatic point of view, the Singaporean leaders deemed Singlish useless, even though it served as a social adhesive, by fostering interaction and a sense of collective identity amongst Singaporeans. Nevertheless, in the eyes of the government, Singlish was a hindrance to the acquisition of 'good English', and so had to be actively discouraged.

> If we speak a corrupted form of English that is not understood by others, we will lose a key competitive edge. My concern is that if we continue to speak Singlish, it will over time become Singapore's common language. Poor English reflects badly on us and makes us seem less intelligent or competent. Investors will hesitate to come over if their managers or supervisors can only guess what our workers are saying. We will find it difficult to be an education and financial centre. Our TV programmes and films will find it hard to succeed in overseas markets because viewers do not understand Singlish. All this will affect our aim to be a first-world economy. (Goh Chok Tong, 2000)

Yet, in 2003, by choosing PCK to front the SARS education music video, the government took the unprecedented step of implicitly endorsing the use of Singlish for public communication to the nation.[6] The SAR-Vivor song lyrics were liberally peppered with Singlish, examples of which included the use of reduplication —

---

6. Compare Hiramoto's (2011) study on a much maligned Hawai'i Creole which got to be used in public discourse.

"don't play play", which means not to play the fool but to be serious; and the use of typical discourse particles such as "ah", "lah" and "leh." (24) in fact, is a meta-linguistic statement on Singaporeans' use of discourse particles; here PCK makes a sociolinguistic observation on the sometimes interchangeable way speakers use the particles "lah" and "leh."

(22)   Think SARS is gone? Your head *ah*.

(23)   Wait a few months *lah*, wait and see. […] Use internet *lah*, use your brain!

(24)   Some say *"leh"*, some say *"lah."*

Another feature of Singlish is the dropping of 's' in verbs that have singular subjects:

(25)   PCK *say* don't play play.

(26)   [It] *Make* me sick when people don't care.

Articles, too, are regularly dropped before nouns, as in:

(27)   Don't be *hero* and continue working.

(28)   Call 993. *Ambulance* will come for free.

Another characteristic of Singlish is its code-mixing between the languages of the major local ethnic communities (viz., Chinese, Malay and Indian) that is also evident in the lyrics:

(29)   Wash your hands whenever you can. […] When you get home, take a bath quickly. *Kiasu* a bit — be safe, not SAR-ry.

(30)   They'll check you up at Tan Tock Seng. Where they know about SARS like I know *Ah Beng*. (*Ah Beng* is a Chinese male proper name that has come to be associated generally with an uncouth, uneducated and unrefined class of men.)

(31)   Don't '*kak-pui!*' all over the place. You might as well *kak-pui* on my face. (A Chinese onomatopoeic word referring to the act of spitting.)

(32)   Hey, if you *kena* Home Quarantine, don't go out except in your dreams. (*kena* is Malay for something (usually unpleasant) that happens to someone.)

(33)   *Tahan* a while and cooperate. (*Tahan* is Malay for to wait or to hold on.)

Apart from lexical borrowings from non-English languages, one encounters also English expressions that are infused with distinctly local meanings:

(34)   *Uncle* Phua says time to fight SARS. (An address term used out of politeness and respect to refer to any older male, not necessarily of kin. For older females, "auntie" is used.)

(35)   You must be *steady*, just use your brain [...]. (An adjective that means cool and ready in any situation (www.singlishdictionary.com))

(36)   Don't be hero and continue working. *Wait* the whole company "kena" quarantine. (Used to refer to a logico-semantic relation of consequence.)

(37)   Think SARS is gone? *Your head* ah. (An exclamation expressing that the person addressed is foolish or talking nonsense (www.singlishdictionary. com))

Although it may appear surprising that the government allowed Singlish to be used in the SARS public education campaign above, it is noteworthy that this was a time of crisis. While seemingly contradicting the government's language ideology, the policy was entirely consonant with the government's broader ideology of pragmatism (see Chua 1995). In line with the latter, it made sense to harness all resources to tackle the immediate threat of the spread of SARS. Once that threat had abated, however, Singlish could once again be relegated to the margins. Still, what had emerged from this episode was the government's begrudging recognition of the importance of Singlish as a community language. If there was a need to reach out urgently and effectively to the masses, then Singlish undeniably had a role to play.[7]

Even so, the government's long-standing position on Singlish vis-à-vis Standard Singapore English had not been seriously compromised by this episode (Lazar 2010). Allowing for Singlish to be used when mediated by PCK in a life-world discourse, implied that the government distanced itself from its actual usage. In fact, even the Singlish in the lyrics was rather temperate. Instead of being wholly in Singlish, a good part of the lyrics was recognizably in Standard English. Note, for example, the following entire stanza:

(38)   Good nutrition and vitamins
        Help you to pass the immunity challenge
        Eat your proteins, carbo and fibre
        Then you can be a 'SAR-vivor.'

In some cases, the Singlish that was performed by PCK in the SARS music video was itself adapted. Two of his earlier infamous catchphrases in the sitcom, "Don't *pray, pray*" and "Use your *blain*" (substituting [r] and [l]), were modified to the

---

7. Chinese 'dialects' were also allowed to be used in public discourse during the SARS period for the same reason. Ordinarily, otherwise, under the Speak Mandarin campaign, the use of other Chinese dialects was actively discouraged.

more 'intelligible' versions "Don't play, play" and "Use your brain" in the lyrics. Compared to the older sitcom PCK, this made the 'new' PCK a good role model for fellow Singaporeans: he evidently had listened to former PM Goh's advice to him in 1999 to make an effort to improve his English. Thus, although not 'perfect' yet from the official standpoint ("Don't play, play" still manifests syntactic reduplication), PCK's English is becoming more intelligible to audiences who would not be familiar with 'hard-core' Singlish. Although made to appear 'real', PCK of course is a fabricated personality without any ability or volition to improve his English. Rather, PCK as spokesperson or mascot of the public campaigns has been adjusted to fit the audience. With regard to the campaigns, he had to be made politically correct insofar as the government's official stance towards English was concerned, and he had to be intelligible to reach a wide range of expected audiences.

If PCK had already begun to show linguistic 'improvement' in 2003, barely three years after Goh's comment, then by 2009 his Singlish was almost entirely on the wane. Reading the printed lyrics of the Courtesy rap that appears in the music video, one would be hard pressed to find traces of Singlish. Only in PCK's articulation of the lyrics, performed in his characteristic manner and accent, is there some use of the discourse particles "ah" and "lah":

(39)   excuse me *ah*, while I give you a kick!

(40)   please move inside, don't block me *lah*.

(41)   Everyone listen. Be gracious. Thank you *ah*.

What the above suggests is that while it is alright for PCK to speak with traces of Singlish — even though now greatly reduced —, viewers who are invited to sing along following the printed lyrics are encouraged to do so in a version devoid of spoken Singlish features. This way, his Singlish-tainted English may be used symbolically to index the lifeworld without radically altering the official language ideology concerning 'good English.' In other words, PCK's symbolic usage of Singlish in public discourse realizes the institutional objective of appealing, and reaching out to ordinary Singaporeans, without overtly endorsing its usage.

4.4 Enacting community

Singlish is a marker par excellence of Singaporean-ness, which makes its presence — even symbolically — integral to the performance of the Singaporean lifeworld. In concert with this, we find other discursive and semiotic strategies that index and build membership in a shared lifeworld. Presupposition of terms and references that are made in the lyrics index common ground, based upon shared knowledge and experiences. Examples from the SARS video include:

(42)   The lexical item "kaya" in "Spread *kaya*, but don't spread SARS!" (kaya is a favorite local spread on toast, referred to here as something commonly understood).

(43)   When PCK refers to himself as "Uncle Phua" (in "*Uncle* Phua says time to fight SARS"), the kinship address term is not out of place for the Singaporean audience, even though PCK is never addressed like that in the sitcom (not even by his nephew). Making reference to himself as "uncle" in the SARS music video, in fact, quite cleverly allows him to derive authority from the lifeworld as someone to be respected in terms of seniority; in this way, it becomes contextually acceptable for him to adopt a somewhat scolding stance. Using a term of familiarity for himself in this way, PCK depicts himself as someone within the community who has authority to address his fellow Singaporeans.

(44)   Reference to "Tan Tock Seng" in "Ambulance will come for free. To check you up at *Tan Tock Seng*" also presupposes that the audience can identify one of the major hospitals in Singapore as the particular hospital reserved during the SARS crisis to (quarantine and) treat (suspected) patients.

(45)   The instructions "Wait at the clinic, stay in one spot. Don't spread your germs at the coffee shop" refers to a well-publicized incident: an irresponsible person infected with SARS had, instead of waiting at the clinic, walked over to a coffee place and could have infected many unsuspecting people. The admonishment-cum-reminder presupposes that all Singaporeans were aware of this case.

A shared lifeworld is also built through usage of inclusive pronouns, such as "we"/ "our" and "you and me", as well as the pronominal forms "everybody"/"everyone." The use of these forms co-opts the audience into a cohesive community with a common goal: to tackle challenges together. As a community, Singaporeans are enjoined to be responsible, civic minded, and mobilized into collective action:

(46)   But *we* can fight this, *you and me*. Help fight SARS in *our* country. (SARS lyrics)

(47)   *Everybody, we* have a part to play. To help fight SARS at the end of the day! (SARS lyrics)

(48)   Think SARS is gone? Your head ah. But listen to me and *we*'ll be ok lah. (SARS lyrics)

(49)   Keep *our* country clean and green. Because nowadays, the germs are mean. (SARS lyrics)

(50)   *Everyone* listen. Be gracious. (Courtesy lyrics)

Further, the choice of the particular music genre as the medium of the campaign messages is well-suited to the lifeworld. Rap music, while not indigenous or dominant on the local music scene, is here infused with a local accent, as in the SARS and Courtesy music videos, thereby engaging the local audience as a community. As noted by some scholars, the transcultural flow of rap music today has resulted in 'localized' versions circulating in various countries around the world; just like hip hop culture more broadly, rap music changes and gets reused so as to fashion new identities (Pennycook and Mitchell, 2009). In the case of the present music videos, this 'localization' of rap in PCK's rendition gives an updated, 'hip' feel to the campaign, adding a twist of levity and humor even while making a serious educational point. At the same time, by its spoken quality, rap enables PCK to tell people what to do (and not do), and achieves this while being set to a lively, catchy and easily remembered rhythm.

The music videos, moreover, are presented karaoke-style, with the lyrics shown at the bottom of the screen. This means that PCK is not simply performing *for* the audience; rather, the audience is invited to join in and rap along with him. Such a sing-along strategy is a clever, entertaining way of involving the audience, while at the same time reinforcing the memorability of the education messages. This communitization-cum-memorability effect on actual audiences can be illustrated by a comment made by the actor Gurmit Singh (who plays PCK in the videos) during the SARS period:

> Everywhere I go, people start shouting at me 'some say leh, some say lah...', and kids keep chanting 'SARS is the virus that I just want to minus...' [...] My friend told me that he's been to the CCs [Community Centres] and groups of children even chanted the SARS rap. People have also requested this song on the airways of Perfect Ten 98.7 FM! (MediaCorp 27 June 2003)

Finally, by performing the rap also in public spaces, PCK both indexes and engages the lifeworld community. That is, the performance of the message is taken out of the music videos shown on television screens, into the lived social spaces of communities of people. During the SARS period, Gurmit Singh, as PCK, went to schools, residential community centers and workplaces to perform the rap and disseminate the educational message, thereby taking media interdiscursivity into the social life of the community. In addition, communities were featured together with PCK in the SARS and Courtesy music videos. For instance, some of the scenes in the SARS video featured groups of people (e.g. drivers of a public transportation company) in the background singing along with PCK. The Courtesy music video itself was set in an MRT train station and on board a train, with PCK interacting with the community of passengers.

5. Summary and conclusion

This article has examined the role of media interdiscursivity in social governance; specifically, how PCK, a popular television character has been appropriated by the Singaporean authorities to achieve the objectives of two national public education campaigns. The appropriation of PCK into the campaign genre rests on his appeal as emblematic of the lifeworld, and all that it entails. The lifeworld, in the article, was discursively analyzed in terms of the dual processes of informalization and communitization, and discussed in relation to the choice of PCK for his ordinariness and 'realness', his informal speech style, his enactment of 'community', and his use of Singlish.

The presence of Singlish is surprising, not because it is a constituent of the lifeworld discourse, but because of its use in public communication by authorities, who have been openly disdainful of it and have launched a counter SGEM campaign that exists concurrently. Yet, its presence in the music videos indicates the authorities' recognition that connection through the lifeworld to the public can be effectively achieved through Singlish. Does this then signal an ideological shift of the government? At the macro ideological level of pragmatism, there is no shift or contradiction. The pragmatism that underlies the government's disparagement of Singlish (because it lacks a use-value in international communication) also underscores tolerance of Singlish in the two national campaigns (because of its function in connecting to the lifeworld). In terms of language ideological shifts, there appears to be periodic suspensions in prescriptivism, in allowing Singlish, via PCK, some space in public discourse. Notably, the implicit acknowledgement of Singlish as the language of the 'community' makes it an appropriate resource to reach out to the general Singaporean public. However, by and large, the government's language ideology pertaining to Singlish vis-à-vis Standard Singapore English remains unchanged. Like the sporadic accommodation of Singlish in the campaigns, the maintenance of the government's official language ideology is also achieved via the interdiscursive appropriation of PCK. Firstly, the presence of Singlish in the national public discourse is mediated by PCK i.e., the language is associated with him and not directly with the authorities. Secondly, in the process of interdiscursivity, the variety of Singlish imported into the campaign communication has been 'cleaned up'. In fact, the language used by PCK in the lyrics is not wholly Singlish, but a Singlish-inflected English, which serves to symbolically connect with the audience, while still maintaining wider intelligibility. Interestingly, compared to the 2003 SARS lyrics, the 2009/10 Courtesy lyrics, as earlier mentioned, is almost devoid of Singlish markers, except for the end-particles inserted by PCK (but not found on the screen). This can be explained in terms of the processes of interdiscursivity and intertextuality. The interdiscursive appropriation from sitcom PCK to spokesperson/mascot PCK in 2003 required a greater importation of Singlish markers, as Singlish was so closely tied to his sitcom character role. However, by 2009/10, the role of PCK as spokesperson/mascot was already established, so that the 'borrowing' wasn't directly from the sitcom necessarily, but intertextually from his earlier public service role. Arguably, therefore, in 2009/10, PCK could be re-appropriated as signifier of the lifeworld, without attaching too much emphasis on the Singlish appeal, although a symbolic semblance of the latter remains.

In concluding, one might ask whether the use of PCK in the public service role has been a successful strategy. From the perspective of the authorities, it would appear that the strategy of media interdiscursivity has allowed the institutional actors — as the idiomatic expression goes — to have their cake and eat it too. Mediated by the voice of the lifeworld, and especially via PCK's voice, the government is able to ride on the earlier popularity of the PCK character and accrue the benefits of adopting a lifeworld discourse. In fact, the campaign messages can continue to be direct, scolding, and didactic (as were the earlier campaign communications by the government), yet not be construed as annoying because the messages are seen as coming personally from a likeable character with social capital, instead of top-down from an impersonal, authoritarian institutional voice of the government. Moreover, the government can utilize, strategically and symbolically, a Singlish-inflected English, while preserving PCK's lifeworld appeal and maintaining the integrity of its official language ideology.

However, from the point of view of audience reception, it is unclear whether — and to what extent — PCK has been a successful public service ambassador in the two national campaigns, and would warrant a separate study altogether. The SAR-Vivor rap, as mentioned, was one of many educational outreach initiatives of the government during the crisis period; still, by Gurmit Singh's own account his performance of the rap in public community spaces was well-received and the public found the lyrics memorable. The 'happy journey starts like that!' courtesy campaign music video is a very recent initiative, and its effectiveness is yet unknown. In any case, addressing the courtesy etiquette of Singaporeans has been a long-standing effort, which is likely to continue for years to come.

There is some recent indication to suggest that the appeal of PCK, the sitcom character — and by implication, the 'recycling' of the character (see Agha, this volume) in his public service role — may be on the wane. At the time of completing this article, *Phua Chu Kang: The Movie* was launched in the local cinemas, following the success of the earlier television series that ended in 2007 in Singapore. A full-page review of the movie was devoted in *The Straits Times Life!*, a section of the main English daily, bearing the following caption:

> Thumbs down for PCK. It is such a joke that Phua Chu Kang should still be around, much less appear in a movie that shows the [Ah] Beng contractor making the same tired jokes. He's back but should anyone care? Gurmit Singh is still hawking tired comedic schtick. (Lui, 2010)

The reviewer remarked that by "refusing to acknowledge his sell-by date, [PCK] went from being cool to being a joke", and recommended that "It is high time Phua Chu Kang had a fatal construction site accident" for the character had "long ago [been] bled dry of any entertainment value." While rather harsh, it is telling that the 'winning PCK formula' has outlived its appeal (at least for this journalist), to which the authorities would need to pay attention in considering PCK's continued relevance as a public service ambassador. Given that the authorities have been mindful of the need to keep the campaign approach fresh, relevant and engaging — indeed, the idea to use PCK originally stemmed from that — it would seem that the task of re-inventing the communication approach, once more, is imminent and will be on-going as long as Singapore continues to remain a campaign country.

Acknowledgement

I thank Mie Hiramoto and the reviewers of this article for their helpful and detailed comments.

References

Anderson, Benedict. 1983/2006. Imagined Communities: Reflections on the origin and spread of nationalism. London: Verso.
Bakhtin, Mikhail. 1986/2006. The Problem of Speech Genres. In: Adam Jaworski and Nikolas Coupland (eds), The Discourse Reader. Second edition. London: Routledge.
Bell, Alan 1991. The Language of News Media. Oxford: Blackwell.
Brown, Penelope and Stephen Levinson. 1987. Politeness: Some universals in language usage. Cambridge: Cambridge University Press.
Chua, Beng Huat. 1995. Communitarian Ideology and Democracy in Singapore. London: Routledge.
Fairclough, Norman. 1992. Discourse and SOCIAL CHANGE. London: Polity.
Fairclough, Norman. 1997. Critical Discourse Analysis: The critical study of language. London: Longman.
Featherstone, Mike. 1991. Consumer Culture and Postmodernism. London: Sage.
Goh, Chok Tong. 1999. Prime Minister's National Day Rally Speech.
Goh, Chok Tong. 2000. Prime Minister's National Day Rally Speech.
Goffman, Erving. 1981. Forms of Talk. Philadelphia: University of Pennsylvania Press.
Gordon, Colin. 1987. The Soul of the Citizen: Max Weber and Michel Foucault on rationality and government. In: Sam Whimster and Scott Lash (eds), Max Weber, rationality and modernity, 293–316. London: Allen and Unwin.

Hiramoto, Mie. 2011. Consuming the Consumers: Semiotics of Hawai'i Creole in advertisements. *Journal of Pidgin and Creole Linguistics* 26, 2, 247–275.

Hu, R.T.T. 1998. Making Courtesy a Way of Life. Speeches. 1998, 22, 4, 25–28.

Lazar, Michelle M. 2000. Gender, Discourse and Semiotics: The politics of parenthood representations. Discourse and Society 11, 3, 373–400.

Lazar, Michelle M. 2003 Semiosis, Social Change and Governance: A critical semiotic analysis of a national campaign. Social Semiotics, 13, 3, 201–221.

Lazar, Michelle M. 2010. Language Ideologies and State Imperatives: The strategic use of Singlish in public media discourse. In: Sally Johnson and Tommaso Milani (eds), Language Ideologies and Media Discourse, 121–142. London: Continuum.

Leong, Hoe Nam et.al. 2006. SARS in Singapore –Predictors of disease severity. PubMed. (http://www.ncbi.n/m.nih.gov/pubmed/16829999)

Lim, Teng Kiat et.al. 2003. Impact of Severe Acute Respiratory Syndrome (SARS) on the Singapore economy. Economic Survey of Singapore First Quarter 2003.
  (http://app-stg.mti.gov.sg/data/article/21/doc/NWS_2003Q1_SARS.pdf)

Lui, John. 2010. Thumbs down for PCK. The Straits Times Life! 11 August.

Menon, K.U. 2006. SARS Revisited: Managing 'outbreaks' with 'communications.' Annals Academy of Medicine, 35, 5, 361–367.

Ministry of Information and the Arts (MITA). 1999. Courtesy: More than a smile. The Singapore Courtesy Council.

Pennycook, Alastair and Mitchell, Tony. 2009. Hip Hop as Dusty Foot Philosophy: Engaging locality. In: H.Samy Alim, Awad Ibrahim and Alastair Pennycook (eds), 2009. Global Linguistic Flows: Hip hop culture, youth identities and the politics of language, 25–42. London: Routledge.

Rose, Nikolas. 1996. Re-figuring the Territory of Government. Economy and Society, 25, 3, 327–356.

Tolson, Andrew. 1991. Televised Chat and the Synthetic Personality. In: Paddy Scannell (ed), Broadcast Talk, 178–200. London: Sage.

van Leeuwen, Theo. 1987. Generic Strategies in Press Journalism, Australian Review of Applied Linguistics, 10, 2, 199–220.

Appendices

1.SAR-Vivor Rap (Lyrics of SARS Rap)

Verse 1:
Some say "leh", some say "lah"
Uncle Phua says time to fight SARS
Everybody, we have a part to play
To help fight SARS at the end of the day.

Wash your hands whenever you can
Wash with soap, then at least got hope
When you get home, take a bath quickly
"Kiasu" a bit — be safe, not "SAR-ry."

Try not to travel to SARS countries
Wait a few months lah, wait and see
Eh why you rush to catch that plane?
Use internet lah, use your brain!

Getting protection from this virus
Means getting healthy- inside us
Don't work too much until you're sick
Get exercise and get yourself fit.

Good nutrition and vitamins
Help you to pass the immunity challenge
Eat your proteins, carbo and fibre
Then you can be a... "SAR-vivor."

PCK say don't play play
or this stupid SARS is here to stay
But we can fight this, you and me
Help fight SARS in our country.

SARS is the virus that I just want to minus
No more surprises if you use your brain, use your brain, use your braaainnn,
Can't SARS me baby, and I don't mean maybe
You must be steady, just use your brain, use your brain, use your braaainnn.

Verse 2:
Some say "leh", some say "lah"
Spread kaya, but don't spread SARS.
Everybody, we have a part to play
To help fight SARS at the end of the day.

If you're sick, don't go to work
Even if your boss is a jerk
Don't be hero and continue working
Wait the whole company "kena" quarantine.

Wear a mask when you see doctor
See the same one, don't be a doc hopper
Wait at the clinic, stay in one spot
Don't spread your germs at the coffee shop.

Think you got SARS? Call 993
Ambulance will come for free
They'll check you up at Tan Tock Seng
Where they know about SARS like I know about "Ah Bengs."

Hey, if you "kenna" Home Quarantine
Don't you go out except in your dreams
"Tahan" a while and cooperate
Don't give everybody a big headache.

PCK say don't play play
or this stupid SARS is here to stay
But we can fight this, you and me
Help fight SARS in our country.

SARS is the virus that I just want to minus
No more surprises if you use your brain, use your brain, use your braaainnn,
Can't SARS me baby, and I don't mean maybe
You must be steady, just use your brain, use your brain, use your braaainnn.

Verse 3:
Some say "leh", some say "lah"
Keep the place clean, and keep out SARS.
Everybody, we have a part to play
To help fight SARS at the end of the day.

Don't throw your tissues all over the shop
Think no one can see you so you don't stop
Make me sick when people don't care
Make you sick when you breathe the air.

Even when things are getting better
Don't do things and become a "regret-ter"
Think SARS is gone? Your head ah.
But listen to me and we'll be ok lah.

PCK say don't play play
or this stupid SARS is here to stay
But we can fight this, you and me
Help fight SARS in our country.

Keep our country clean and green
Because nowadays, the germs are mean
Don't leave food for stray dogs or cats
Unless you want to keep their germs as pets.

Cover your mouth if you cough or sneeze
You think everyone want to catch your disease?
Don't "kak-pui"! all over the place
You might as well "kak pui" on my face.

SARS is the virus that I just want to minus
No more surprises if you use your brain, use your brain, use your braaainnn,
Can't SARS me baby, and I don't mean maybe
You must be steady, just use your brain, use your brain, use your braaainnn.

2. A Happy Journey Starts Like That (Lyrics of Courtesy Rap)

Verse 1:
Hey you, over there
Don't cut queue, don't you dare.
Wait your turn to board the train
What's the rush? There's no rain!

Verse 2:
Hey you, pretending to sleep
Nodding and drooling on the reserved seat.
Not pregnant, old or really in need.
Excuse me (ah), while I give you a kick!

Verse 3:
Hey you, standing there.
Next to the door without a care.
There's space behind, can't you see?
Please see inside, don't block me (lah).

Verse 4 (repeated twice)
Before you go in, let them out.
Before you sit, look around.
Just got on? Move to the back.
A happy journey starts like that.
Everyone listen. Be gracious.
Thank you (ah). Bye!

Recycling mediatized personae across participation frameworks*

Asif Agha
University of Pennsylvania

1. Introduction

The papers in this volume discuss forms of semiotic mediation that unfold through mediatized texts (newspapers, anime, movies, reality TV), focusing especially on diacritics of social personae that are animated and re-animated through textual encounters.[1] It is therefore useful to locate these papers at the intersection of three questions:

(1) How do mediatized texts make social personae available to audiences?

(2) How are these personae recycled from prior discourses into mediatized texts?

(3) How are they recycled into activity frames in social life?

2. Audiences and target markets

The first question requires attention to the target market design of the mediatized text. Any mediatized artifact is a commodity designed for sale to a target market. It also has a textual design, a genre organization and an addressivity to an audience. For instance, the Japanese anime series *Cowboy Bebop* (Hiramoto) is of an entertainment genre targeted to young heterosexual adults. It employs everyday registers of Japanese as elements of character design and, by troping on the stereotypic values of register fractions, formulates hybrid personae designed to appeal

---

* Discussant's comments on papers presented in the panel "Media intertextualities: Semiotic Mediation across time and space," 108th annual meeting, American Anthropological Association, Philadelphia, December 5, 2009

1. See list of paper titles and authors at the end of this document.

to its young audience. By contrast, the Korean news genre on which Park focuses, "English learning success stories," formulates the English language as a commodity register for Koreans by linking English to occupational and commercial success in Korea (Agha in press). The newspapers in which the news genre occurs are conservative national dailies with a 75% market share of the news readership; they are oriented to elite commercial interests and the nation's competitiveness in the global economy. The news genre is a mediatized metadiscourse which assigns a foreign language a market value in Korea, and formulates it as a stereotypic indexical of class distinction. Metapragmatic typifications (phrases like "legitimate English" or "high quality English") are used to describe proficiency in English through success stories of register attainment by Korean elites, thus linking ownership of the commodity to achievable occupational positions, formulating English as an instrument of class mobility in Korea.

How is the exemplary Korean speaker of English typified in this mediatized genre? Through news stories. For whom? For newspaper readers. What do these news stories do? They contain narrated speech events. What happens in them? Metapragmatic typifications abound in which a narrated character, the "featured learner," is formulated *both* as *high-ranking Korean* and as *exemplary speaker of English*. For example, in the narrated speech event in which Ms. Barshefsky is represented as asking Mr. Han "where did you learn such high quality English?," the ventriloquated question formulates Mr. Han as an exemplary speaker for a newspaper readership. Rank asymmetries in the narrated speech event diagram rank asymmetries in the event of newspaper reading. Ms. Barshefsky out-ranks Mr. Han by criteria of native speaker proficiency, and Mr. Han out-ranks most readers by criteria of professional attainment. When she formulates him as a speaker of high-quality English, her native proficiency confers legitimacy on his attained proficiency. He is now available as an exemplary persona for the newspaper reader, at once a model of linguistic and occupational attainment.

In discussing the newspaper texts through which this register formulation becomes known to a population of speakers, Park focuses only on a phase or segment of the social process through which this register has a social life in Korea, a phase analogous to the 19th century formulation of British Received Pronunciation (RP) as a register of class mobility in England through mediatized texts such as Newspapers and Penny Weeklies (Agha 2007, ch. 4). As I show in the RP case, considering the larger speech chain process helps us see that exemplary speakers, repertoires, enregistered values, and the social domain of enregisterment were all transformed over a historical process through the activities of social persons linked to each other through it. Although Park does not discuss the diverse social settings in which "good English" functions as a social indexical in Korean society, he does make clear how a single mediatized genre personifies English (and its

Korean users) within a space of characterological contrasts. These personae are potentially available for uptake and recycling in subsequent activities in social life.

But what happens off the page? How do depictions of rank in the news genre inform class asymmetries in Korean society? As in the British case of RP, class structure is here reproduced asymmetrically through a commodity chain. Although English is commoditized as a register of white collar job placement in Korea, and although this indexical value becomes known to anyone who reads the paper, the valued commodity is only purchasable by attending language schools. Although the newspaper genre locates Korean personae associated with exemplary English within a classification of social types — they contrast, for instance, with defective personae associated with those who speak Konglish (a blend of Korean and English) — no reader can, of course, learn good English through news stories written in Korean. The competence to speak in this register requires appropriate English language schooling. Park notes that such schooling is "prohibitively costly for working class families and even for middle class families." Fluency in the register thus remains a restricted commodity, recognized as valuable (through newspapers) by more people than can afford it (through schooling). A class structure is potentially reproduced and maintained through an emblem of class distinction. And insofar as the emblem is associated with English, local social aspirations to success (of those who seek employment) are linked to global economic aspirations (of those who provide it). Figurements of linguistic and professional competence within Korea are thereby incorporated in a trans-local neoliberal imaginary, and local participation frameworks (and the aspirations that unfold within them) are assimilated into more global commodity chains.

3.   Troping on stereotypic inputs

Let us now turn to the second question: How are social personae recycled into mediatized texts from prior discourses? The Singaporean case discussed by Lazar provides an interesting contrast to the Japanese case discussed by Hiramoto.

In the case discussed by Hiramoto, register and dialect contrasts within everyday spoken Japanese are important source materials in mediatized depictions of social personae. The discursive elements of character design in *Cowboy Bebop* are Japanese speech registers that index nation, class, and gender contrasts (Standard Japanese, men's language, women's language respectively), as well as regional dialects that are enregistered in that national imaginary as extra-normative in contrast to Standard Japanese, and thus contrastively linked to sub-standard social personae (rural vs. urban, working class vs. middle class, less vs. more educated people). These register contrasts are troped upon in various ways in the mediatized text, but we cannot understand the significance of these mediatized tropes without first noting that registers are inputs to tropes in non-mediatized discourses too.

I have argued elsewhere that any register routinely provides inputs to tropes in everyday life (Agha 2007, ch. 3): Uses of women's registers by men, or of adult speech by children (or vice versa), or of honorific registers in acts of veiled aggression are cross-linguistically commonplace as entextualized tropes, even though indexical stereotypes associated with source registers are often taken to imply — particularly in decontextualized reflection about lexemic fragments of a register — that such language use does not occur, or occurs only in the speech of stigmatized others (Agha 1998).

In *Cowboy Bebop*, register mediated tropes become instruments of **character design**: contrasts among registers motivate social-interpersonal contrasts among the anime's characters. Main protagonists speak Standard Japanese, side characters are assigned non-Standard dialects and non-normative personae. The register called *Hakasego* 'scientist speech' is used for knowledgeable old men unless they are villains or foreigners. Foreigners are differentiated further by similar techniques: Japanese disfluency plus Chinese word borrowings index a Chinese character (the bartender), English borrowings typical of the register of *Seiyôjingo* 'westerner's language' formulate a character like Andy as "Caucasian"; and stereotypically Native American idioms and locutionary styles animate the othering of the medicine man (Laughing Bull).

The Singaporean case discussed by Lazar highlights the role of institutional value projects in formulating texts that recycle social personae. The Singaporean state routinely employs public relations methods to pursue campaigns of "public education" through diverse mediatized texts that are delivered to the public via venues such as TV, and are designed to promote specific outcomes in diverse areas of everyday life. In the two campaigns she discusses — one on public health, one on courtesy in public life — Lazar focuses on the incorporation into textual design of a particular media personality, a television character named Phua Chu Kang (PCK), who becomes an intermediary of the State's public relations efforts. How is this persona constituted and deployed? He is known as a comical figure from the sitcom that originally brought him to national prominence. And he has a narrow register range, speaking always in an informal conversational style, regardless of the social setting in which he finds himself. He also speaks Singlish, a colloquial variety of Singaporean English (with borrowings from Malay and Chinese), which is heavily stigmatized in other campaigns through which the Singaporean State seeks to promote Standard English.

When PCK's colloquial persona is preserved in the State's "public courtesy" campaign, he is formulated as an ordinary, everyday person, and this formulation bespeaks a particular addressee design. He speaks for the State as a spokesman for its public courtesy campaign, but not in the voice of the State. Rather than speaking as the State does to its subjects (in Standard English), he speaks in a vernacular and colloquial English, peppered with Singlish, in which members of the public can imagine themselves speaking to each other. One participation framework re-animates the discursive design (and personae) of another. But when he speaks Singlish while speaking for the State, does he not undermine the State's Standard language policy?

The way in which Singlish is recycled into his speech prevents this effect, and does so in two ways. First, the lexical and stylistic repertoires of Singlish are greatly muted and reduced when he speaks — or, rather, sings — for the courtesy campaign's music video. This reduced and fragmentary Singlish suffices to index the voice of the public to the public, though this voice is also muted here by the relative infrequency of Singlish tokens (compared to actual everyday speech). Second, Singlish is fragmentarily preserved in addressee design, but not at all in replication design. The lyrics of the music video are designed to be repeated by viewers who are invited to sing along. But the text-segments of the video that viewers are invited to reproduce through their own singing contains no Singlish whatsoever. They are to sing in Standard English. The music video is a State-sponsored mediatized text whose addressee design is based on recycling everyday speech and its personae. But in modeling the subsequent behavior of its addressees, it ventriloquates onto their lips personae that are sponsored by the State.

4.   Uptake in social interaction

Tropic transformations refashion social possibilities by creating new inputs to uptake. Hiramoto notes that *Cowboy Bebop*'s main protagonists are given Standard Japanese voices, even if they are Singapore-born (Faye), or working class (V.T). The anime's textual form therefore links Standard Japanese to social categories of which it is not stereotypically indexical. When it is used by the anime's main protagonists, Standard Japanese is linked to their *other* visible and audible characteristics, and hence to their co-textually configured personae (Agha 2007: 159–165), some of which (foreign birth, low class) are simply inconsistent with widespread stereotypes about the Standard Language, while others (bounty hunting, violence, ambiguous gender) are actually stigmatized by adult speakers of the Standard. The mediatized text's character design formulates its indexical selectivity for a distinct — younger — target market: Three of the four main characters are young people, whose presence in the anime formulates its addressivity to a teenage or twenty-something audience. Standard Japanese provides a figurement of normality to characters who are extra-normative from the standpoint of adult society, but altogether "cool" in entertainment genres designed for the anime's target market, which includes young people of the urban (Tokyo) middle class. The figurement of young bounty hunters speaking Standard Japanese, which is stereotypically spoken best in Tokyo, is therefore a highly motivated trope of addressee design. Since enregistered voices are only encountered as fragments of entextualized voices (Agha 2005), entextualized tropes of these kinds open up new possibilities for uptake and response in everyday life too.

How do members of the target market recycle *Cowboy Bebop* personae in their own activities? We don't know because Hiramoto does not explore this issue in her discussion. But let us at least consider what is *made available for uptake* by these tropic formulations. What can be recycled here is not just the idea that Standard Japanese is a hegemonic standard but also the extra-normative aspects of its anime speakers (e.g., Ed's gender ambiguity, Faye's con-artist persona, addiction to gambling and penchant for street-fighting). And recycling is not reducible to "imitation." Indeed, the ways in which these personae can be recycled include (1) activities like performing persona fractions by performing register fragments; (2) activities like performing counter-persona and hybrid analogues through entextualized tropes; and (3) activities that depend not on deploying such personae but on *talking about them*, as when talk about mediatized characters enables forms of interpersonal footing in everyday life, e.g., in talk of why one loves or hates Ed and someone else doesn't, why one would never want one's best friend to be like Spike, and so on.

The question of how mediatized personae are recycled into subsequent discourses emerges in the papers by Furukawa and by Wahl. Despite apparent differences of content, both papers explore the recycling of stereotypic personae from source discourses into interactional tropes that yield footings and alignments among current participants.

Let's begin with Furukawa's paper. Although most media research confines itself to so-called "content analysis" of media texts, Furukawa discusses interpersonal alignments between media personae and those who respond to them as viewers or hearers. One of the media texts that Furukawa investigates is a comedy skit by Augie T, originally performed at a hotel in Honolulu before an audience of 70–80 people. The comedy routine animates ethnic personae that are sourced from racial stereotypes and made available as ethnic humor. Furukuwa's paper describes the subsequent metapragmatic commentary on this skit by participants in a focus group. The issue of ethnicity is flagged by the comedy skit itself. What is interesting here, however, is the reluctance of the focus group participants to discuss their own views of racially charged ethnic humor, and their approach to getting around needing to do so.

When these Hawaii residents, who are not themselves black, are asked about their views on ethnic humor, a mediatized figure — Barack Obama — is conjured as the imaginary respondent to this question, a figure safely distinct — and corporeally distant — from the focus group participants who animate it. But Obama must first himself be reformulated before his ventriloquated opinions about ethnic humor can be pressed into service. He is reformulated from being a *biographic individual* into a *social character type* (Agha 2005), one from whom most features of his biographic individuality are effaced (the lawyer, the social worker, the president) and only two features, namely his ethnicity and his "local boy" aspect, are left salient. These are precisely those fragments of the Obama persona that are most relevant to ventriloquating him as respondent to the question. His ethnicity is convenient because if a black man is likely to enjoy racial humor, it is safe for white people to do so. His locale-specificity is convenient because if someone who lived in Hawaii for many years (such as himself) can enjoy such humor, anyone having the same category membership (the same locale specificity) can safely enjoy it too. This allows the focus group members (who share his locale specificity but not his race) to avoid answering the question themselves; they are able, instead, to animate a character type who enjoys it, and by using fragments of the Obama persona to formulate the character type, they are able to align themselves with the character type they animate, without fully inhabiting it.

If Furukawa discusses uptake of mediatized texts by focus groups, Wahl discusses uptake in subsequent mediatized texts. And just as Furukawa's respondents transform the figures they recycle, so do the characters in the films and reality TV shows discussed by Wahl.

The case which Wahl discusses involves personae sourced from American youth slang and from mediatized texts (films) that recycle such slang in the service of character depiction, making versions of it widely known through their own dissemination. What Wahl calls "metastereotyping" is a cyclic recontextualization of enregistered diacritics and personae (Agha 2007, ch. 5) across participation frameworks, of which Wahl discusses three. There is the 'cool' of American youth slang, a register of peer-group footing in the US, which changes very rapidly; there is the mediatized speech of the main characters in *Bill and Ted's Excellent Adventure*, who make a small sample of such youth slang internationally known in the 1990s, thus transforming the social regularity in its most widely known form — by reducing its repertoires (to fragments of US slang), expanding its social domain (the film has a global market), and adding to its stereotypic personae (which now include Bill and Ted); and, finally, there is Rico and Munya in Africa, on reality TV, putting mediatized Bill and Ted characters — and the slang sourced from them, which they transform, again, in repertoire and persona characteristics — to good interpersonal use.

Bill and Ted's "California slacker youth" (along with analogues like *Ridgemont High's* "surfer dude") are stereotypic personae well known among American youth populations and elsewhere. Bill and Ted have many virtues, but being super-smart is not among them. What's very useful about them, however, is that they are mediatized figures linked to linguistic and kinesic repertoires. They can thus be re-animated by performing them.

Rico and Munya do the same when they attempt to seem attractive to Hazel, who states plainly that she doesn't date "men who are too smart." In their concerted effort to achieve performed dim-wittedness for Hazel's hand, Rico and Munya find that Bill and Ted are handy source personae indeed — though most features of their biographic individuality (as movie characters) are now irrelevant. What is relevant is Bill and Ted's speech and demeanor, and their stereotypically dim-witted personae, which are hyper-stylized in Rico and Munya's performance with back-to-back tokens of "dude" for Hazel's benefit, even if, as they appear to concede, their efforts at dim-wittedness fall short of getting a date.

Once we see that the repertoires associated with register models of speech and other conduct include semiotically *diverse* signs (lexemes, speech styles, kinesic demeanors, etc.), whose social domain is mediated by indexical stereotypes, including those circulated through mediatized discourses, register models and their tropic deployments become socially locatable as objects of ethnographic investigation. And ethnographic observation makes plain that the co-existence of distinct models of the same repertoire is not only routine everywhere, but the transformation of models and the competition between variant models within and across activity frames is the very stuff of social life.

Papers under commentary

Furukawa, Toshiaki. 'Intertextuality, mediation, and members' categories in focus groups on humor.'

Hiramoto, Mie. 'Anime and intertextualities: Hegemonic identities in *Cowboy Bebop*'

Lazar, Michelle M. 'Performing the "lifeworld" in public education campaigns: Media interdiscursivity and social governance.'

Park, Joseph S. 'Images of "good English" in the Korean conservative press: Three processes of interdiscursivity.'

Wahl, Alexander. 'The global metastereotyping of Hollywood 'Dudes': African reality television parodies of mediatized California style.'

References

Agha, Asif. 1998. 'Stereotypes and registers of honorific language.' Language in Society, 27, 2, 151–194.

Agha, Asif. 2005. 'Voice, footing, enregisterment.' Journal of Linguistic Anthropology, 15, 1, 38–59.

Agha, Asif. 2007. Language and Social Relations. Cambridge: Cambridge University Press.

Agha, Asif. in press. 'Commodity registers'. To appear in Journal of Linguistic Anthropology, Spring 2011.

Index